D1068305

THE ETHICS OF OUR CLIMATE
Hermeneutics and Ethical Theory

THE ETHICS OF OUR CLIMATE
Hermeneutics and Ethical Theory

William R. O'Neill, S.J.

GEORGETOWN UNIVERSITY PRESS / WASHINGTON, D.C.

To my family

BJ1031
.O54
1994

Georgetown University Press, Washington, D.C.
© 1994 by Georgetown University Press. All rights reserved.
Printed in the United States of America
10 9 8 7 6 5 4 3 2 1   1994

THIS VOLUME IS PRINTED ON ACID-FREE OFFSET BOOK PAPER

Library of Congress Cataloging-in-Publication Data

O'Neill, William R.
   The ethics of our climate : hermeneutics and ethical theory /
William R. O'Neill.
      p. cm.
   Includes bibliographical references.
   1. Ethics. 2. Ethics, Modern—20th century. 3. Hermeneutics.
4. Postmodernism.   I. Title.
BJ1031.054 1994
171—dc20
ISBN 0-87840-565-8   94-11004

Contents

Preface

"'Tis all in pieces" writes the poet John Donne of the "frailty and decay of this whole world." For virtue and verity are "things forgot" as "new philosophy calls all in doubt."[1] Donne's "Anatomy" of the modern world is somber, yet prescient, for the tragedies of our own day belie the Kantian ideal of an ethical commonwealth. One wonders, indeed, if we have not built a new Babel, for our differences seem insuperable and moral theory of little avail: Kant's "formalism" proves empty, and neo-Aristotelian ethics blind—even religious ethics succumbs to modernity's grammar of dissent.

In these pages, I seek to chart a via media between these extremes, for moral wisdom is gleaned, I believe, in the very genealogy of our differences. The historical criticism of Aristotelian and Kantian moral theories in Part One sets the stage for a critical appraisal of the rival neo-Kantian theories of R. M. Hare and John Rawls in Part Two. In my criticism of Hans-Georg Gadamer's recovery of Aristotelian *phronēsis* in Part Three, I defend a conception of moral wisdom at play in our ordinary discourse. The final chapter is devoted to assessing the moral import of religious (Christian) belief, for the antinomy of an "empty" formalism (*Moralität*) and "blind" ethics (*Sittlichkeit*) recurs in the dispute of the "autonomy school" and "faith ethic" in modern moral theology. Our hermeneutical reflections may thus be read as a prolegomenon to an ethics which, as befits our (post)modern age, is at once truly Christian and of "our climate."

I wish to express my gratitude to Professor Louis Dupré, whose guidance and criticism have been invaluable in the course of my writing. His inspiration and I hope his wisdom are reflected in these

---

1. John Donne, "An Anatomy of the World," in *The Complete English Poems*, ed. A. J. Smith (New York: Penguin Books, 1971), 276.

pages. I am grateful, likewise, to Professors Margaret Farley and Gene Outka for their kind and judicious criticism, and to Professor Robert Bellah with whom I studied Jürgen Habermas. To these, my mentors and friends, I owe a great debt of gratitude. A Newcombe Fellowship permitted me to complete my dissertation, which has been considerably revised to form the present book, and I thank the Woodrow Wilson Fellowship Foundation for this honor. Finally, I am grateful to Dr. John Samples and Patricia Rayner of Georgetown University Press for their diligent labors in preparing the final manuscript for publication.

Introduction

"When philosophy paints its grey in grey, then has a form of life grown old."[1]

G. W. F. HEGEL

Already the figure is poignant, of wisdom likened by Hegel to the owl of Minerva, who "spreads its wings only with the falling of the dusk."[2] Yet the epiphany is elusive, the illumination tardy. Our musings seem a chronicle of time without event; and like Vladimir and Estragon, beguiled into speech, we wonder, "In all that what truth will there be?"[3] So our moral speech poses itself as a question, a fall from *logos* when all senses serve, yet none is true.

Beckett's tragicomedy is, one might say, a fable of modern morality, where the emissaries of reason are spare and cryptic, like Godot's. Chary in prescribing for her practical office, reason offers her dramatis personae the form of consistency divested of content. There is no startling revelation of duty, nor categorical (apodictic) imperative attesting "the sublimity of our own supersensuous existence."[4]

Morality seems chimerical, for the merely formal determination of volition implied by prudence favors no specifically moral content. One is not necessarily inconsistent in desiring that "others will not do to one what one proposes to do to them." Seeing "no reason to obey its rules," one may reject morality and "be convicted of villainy," writes Philippa Foot, "but not of inconsistency. Nor will [one's] actions necessarily be irrational," since irrationality implies acting so as to defeat one's purposes or ends. "Immorality does not necessarily involve any such thing."[5]

1

Foot's criticism is not a subtle brief for villainy; its gravamen is rather that morality must itself be conceived as "a system of hypothetical imperatives," deriving its justification from the "subjectively and conditionally necessary" aims of social living.[6] Yet if there is no "gradual unveiling, through the use of 'reason', of 'principle' or 'rights' or 'values'"—if such claims, in Richard Rorty's words, are but "edifying" rhetoric, the "poetic achievement" of "'radically situated' individuals and communities"—one wonders, with Nietzsche, if "skepticism regarding morality" is not finally "decisive."[7]

Must we, like Vladimir and Estragon, resign ourselves to "the end of the moral interpretation of the world"—a world, in Nietzsche's words, "which no longer has any sanction after it has tried to escape into some beyond"?[8] And yet if moral skepticism is decisive, it is so only if we assume that morality *must* "escape into some beyond" for its justification. In these pages, I will question the Kantian assumption that morality must be justified by "pure reason alone independently of all experience."[9] The three parts of the book treat of (I) the eclipse of the classical conception of practical reason (*phronēsis*), (II) the Kantian heritage in modern moral theory, and (III) the hermeneutical retrieval of a "moral interpretation of the world."

Our reflections commence with an analysis in chapter 1 of the Aristotelian conception of prudence (*phronēsis*) as "practical wisdom." For Aristotle, *phronēsis* represents a distinctive form of ethical reasoning, skirting the Scylla of abstract formalism (the assimilation of *phronēsis* to *epistēmē*) and the Charybdis of sophistic relativism (the reduction of *phronēsis* to *technē*). The Aristotelian *phronimos* intends virtue for its own sake, as an excellence (*aretē*) of the perfect community (*koinōnia teleios*).

For Kant, however, morality is spun of rarer stuff. Unravelling the rich social tapestry of the *polis* and the City of God, Reason, like Penelope, spins the new morality of freedom's inner law. The social world was divested of the "unwritten, unalterable laws of God and heaven" invoked by Antigone, so that morality might have a surer foundation in Reason.[10] No longer could one assume that the fruition of prudence was the universal good, for the moral law (of Kantian *Moralität*) is justified in abstraction from the "flawed words and stubborn sounds" of virtue:[11] the "*ratio essendi*" of the moral law is the "transcendental freedom" of practically rational agents comprising a purely notional "kingdom of ends."[12]

Kant's belief that morality is illusory if it fails to be so justified would, however, prove to be Janus-faced. As the mind's eye turned inwardly in "respectful doubt," morality itself seemed a making without measure.[13] As I argue in chapter 2, Kant's interpretation of autonomy offers neither a necessary nor a sufficient justification of morality. Practical legislation does not necessarily imply that maxims be given the (universal) form of moral law, nor does the formal stipulation of universalizability suffice to discriminate moral from immoral maxims.

Kant thus bequeaths us a dubious heritage.[14] For, as I argue in Part Two, his modern heirs must found morality upon the very hypothetical imperatives Kant denounced as "vain illusion and splendid misery." For such modern writers as R. M. Hare and John Rawls, whose theories are treated in chapters 3 and 4 respectively, moral imperatives admit of no a priori rational legitimation. Our moral precepts are obliquely derived from a harmony of prudential interests subject to formal, metaethical constraints. Morality becomes a supreme fiction, "constructed" through the imposition of the constraints of impartiality or universalizability upon hypothetical choice.

We are not logically compelled to be moral, nor are our preferences antecedently limited by the ethical (*sittlich*) finality of the virtuous community.[15] The "mutually disinterested rationality" of Rawls's "Kantian constructivism" presumes that "persons in the original position . . . take no interest in one another's interests," while, for the "Kantian utilitarianism" of Hare, "the effect of universalizability is to compel us to find principles" impartially maximizing the satisfaction of preferences—"it does not constrain the preferences themselves."[16] Yet the normative interpretations of either theory, I argue, depend less upon the formal, metaethical stipulations of impartiality or universalizability than upon their differing interpretations of moral *experience* (i.e., the "material" rather than the "formal" construal of the supreme moral law).

Part Three is devoted to a critical retrieval of the conception of prudence. In light of our reflections upon Aristotelian *phronēsis*, I argue in chapter 5 that my prudential prescriptions do not descend from the empyrean as a form of *epistēmē* nor are they reducible to instrumental reasoning or *technē*. Rather, the conative propositional attitude expressed in practical judgment exhibits my formally generalized interest that a rational agent 'S' act in accordance with her best reasons, all things considered, i.e., that 'S' act rationally (prudently).

As my interest, delimiting my self-knowledge as a rationally autonomous prescriber, is logically prior to the reasons rationalizing my action, it forms the intensional context of their interpretation. The formation of my reasons is thus governed by my antecedent interest in (or respect for) the "moral community" of rational (prudential) agents.

Chapter 6 is devoted to resolving a perplexity raised by the foregoing critique of prudence, i.e., that the objectivity of prudential judgments is relative to the "experience" or moral "self-knowledge" of the prescriber. Drawing upon the hermeneutical theory of Hans-Georg Gadamer and the hermeneutical critique of Jürgen Habermas, I contend that the objectivity of practical judgments need not imply our abstraction from the interest or "prejudice" characterizing rational prescribers. For Gadamer, indeed, all such "phronetic" judgments in the human or moral sciences are characterized by our pre-understanding or prejudice, reflecting the "affinity" of knower and known. In the practical realm, autonomy, I will argue, presupposes the affinity of rational prescribers to a possible moral community (a phronetic reconstruction of Kant's "kingdom of ends"). Our reconstruction of Gadamer's appropriation of *phronēsis* thus permits us to understand how our "knowledge of the good" (as expressed in our intentional action descriptions) is determined by our "self-knowledge" as autonomous prescribers (thereby incorporating Habermas's critique in hermeneutical theory).

A final chapter, entitled "A Concluding Theological Postscript," applies our hermeneutical critique to the question of the distinctiveness of Christian ethics. For "disenchantment" with Kantian *Moralität* inspires not only Rorty's liberal irony, but distinctively religious accounts of morality. Proponents of a "faith ethic" (*Glaubensethik*) thus oppose the transcendental methodology of Karl Rahner and his disciples, Bruno Schüller and Josef Fuchs: for Hans Urs von Balthasar, as for Karl Barth, there is no vestibule to moral theology, no purely a priori, transcendental justification of an "anthropological" morality that would render Revelation nugatory.

As I will argue, however, one may concur with Barth and von Balthasar's critique of transcendental moral epistemology yet still uphold an "anthropological" (universal) morality that respects the Christian *proprium*. In reinterpreting Rahner's methodology from a hermeneutical point of view, I contend that the "natural" moral philosophy of the autonomy school need not, in Barth's words, represent an "armistice with the peoples of Canaan."[17] For morality arises not in the pristine certitude of transcendental reflection nor in the "azure silence" of Nietzsche's haven. Our aerie is this world, the "imperfect paradise" in whose "flawed words and stubborn sounds" we find the ethics of our climate.[18]

NOTES TO INTRODUCTION

1. G. W. F. Hegel, *Hegel's Philosophy of Right*, trans. T. M. Knox (Oxford: Oxford University Press, 1952), 13.

2. Ibid.

3. Samuel Beckett, *Waiting for Godot* (New York: Grove Press, 1954), 58.

4. Immanuel Kant, *Critique of Practical Reason*, trans. Lewis White Beck (Indianapolis: Bobbs-Merrill, 1956), 89 (pagination is that of the Prussian Academy edition, vol. 5).

5. Philippa Foot, "Morality as a System of Hypothetical Imperatives," in *Virtues and Vices* (Oxford: Basil Blackwell, 1978), 161–62.

6. Ibid., 170.

7. Richard Rorty, "The Priority of Democracy to Philosophy," in *Prospects for a Common Morality*, ed. Gene Outka and John Reeder (Princeton: Princeton University Press, 1993), 264; Friedrich Nietzsche, *The Will to Power*, bk. 1, trans. W. Kaufmann in *Existentialism from Dostoevsky to Sartre* (New York: Meridian Books, 1956), 110.

8. Nietzsche, *The Will to Power*, 110.

9. Immanuel Kant, *Groundwork of the Metaphysic of Morals*, trans. H. J. Paton (New York: Harper and Row, 1964), 409 (30) (pagination is that of the Prussian Academy edition, vol. 4, while the number in parentheses refers to the second edition of Kant's *Grundlegung zur Metaphysic der Sitten*).

10. Sophocles *Antigone*, in *The Theban Plays*, trans. E. F. Watling (Baltimore: Penguin Books, 1947), lines 555–561, p. 138.

11. Wallace Stevens, "The Poems of Our Climate," in *The Palm at the End of the Mind*, ed. Holly Stevens (New York: Vintage Books, a Division of Random House, 1971), 158.

12. Kant, *Critique of Practical Reason*, 4, n. 1.

13. Jean-Jacques Rousseau, *The Creed of a Priest of Savoy*, trans. Arthur H. Beattie, 2d ed. (New York: Frederick Ungar, 1957), 72. The allusion is to Pico della Mirandola's *Oration on the Dignity of Man*, as quoted in P. O. Kristeller, "The Philosophy of Man in the Italian Renaissance," *Italica* 24 (1947): 100–101.

14. Cf. Louis Dupré, *A Dubious Heritage: Studies in the Philosophy of Religion after Kant* (New York: Paulist Press, 1977), 1–177.

15. John L. Mackie, *Ethics: Inventing Right and Wrong* (Harmondsworth, England: Penguin, 1978), 100.

16. John Rawls, *A Theory of Justice* (Cambridge: Harvard University Press, Belknap Press, 1971), 147; R. M. Hare, *Moral Thinking* (Oxford: Clarendon Press, 1981), 226.

17. Karl Barth, *Church Dogmatics*, II/2, trans. G. W. Bromiley, J. C. Campbell, Iain Wilson, J. Strathearn McNab, Harold Knight, and R. A. Stewart (Edinburgh: T. and T. Clark, 1957), 524.

18. Stevens, "The Poems of Our Climate," 158.

PART ONE

The Eclipse of **Phronēsis**

Part One is devoted to a comparative critique of the Aristotelian and Kantian theories of practical (moral) reasoning. For whether "skepticism regarding morality" is "decisive" depends upon the conception of morality we invoke. The Kantian apotheosis of *Moralität*, I wish to argue, misconstrues Aristotle's understanding of *phronēsis* and so invests Nietzsche's skepticism with its particular force. Our reflections in Part One thus set the stage for our subsequent assessment, in Part Two of the Kantian heritage in modern moral theory.

1

Art and Aretē

"Ah, is there any wisdom in the world?"[1]

SOPHOCLES

Whatever is "right and laudable" for Plato's Protagoras varies with the prevailing sentiments of the *polis*.[2] As the currency of political expedience, Sophistic virtue (*aretē*) is an art or skill, a *technē* that can be taught. Yet for Aristotle, the customary provenance of virtue is entirely consistent with its "natural" character. Opposing a technical reduction of practical reason, Aristotle distinguishes the intellectual (dianoetic) virtue of *phronēsis* from theoretical and technical reasoning. For *phronēsis* is "practical wisdom," aiming at the perfection not of an art but of the *phronimos*. For the Aristotelian *phronimos*, (i) virtuous activity is desired for its own sake, (ii) as an excellence (*aretē*) of the perfect community.

VIRTUOUS ACTIVITY IS DESIRED FOR ITS OWN SAKE

While, according to Aristotle, "the highest possibility of awareness, which the Greeks called *nous* (intellection), is to be attributed to that theoretical knowing which has attained complete self-fulfillment—to *sophia* (wisdom)," the same "highest awareness," writes Gadamer, "is to be attributed to practical reason as well—namely to *phronēsis*, which in each instance is conscious of the rightness of its choice and decision."[3] Yet prudence (*phronēsis*) cannot be conceived as a form of deductive theoretical knowledge (*epistēmē*), for, as Aristotle observes,

9

it apprehends the last step . . . since the thing to be done is of
this nature. Thus it is opposite to intuition [theoretic *nous*]; for
intuition apprehends the definitions, which cannot be logically
demonstrated; and prudence apprehends the ultimate particular,
which cannot be apprehended by scientific knowledge, but only
by perception—not that of objects peculiar to one sense, but the
sort by which we perceive that the ultimate figure in mathematics
is a triangle.[4]

The analogy of practical wisdom with technical expertise in the
Socratic-Platonic tradition is likewise developed by Aristotle inasmuch
as "the originative causes" of action (*praxis*) and production (*poiēsis*)
are variable and contingent. Yet action is generically distinct, "for
production aims at an end other than itself; but this is impossible in the
case of action, because the end is merely doing well."[5] For Aristotle,
apprehension of the "ultimate particular" shows forth "knowledge of
the good for oneself."[6] The "highest awareness" perfecting *phronēsis*
is a form of moral "self-knowledge" mediated in the ultimate particularity of *praxis*, and thus distinguished from theoretical and technical
knowledge alike.[7]

As implied in Aristotle's distinction of the *phronimos* from the
merely clever (*deinos*) agent, who is equally adept at pursuing "unscru-
pulous" ends, *phronēsis* is ordered to the "end and highest good."[8]
Yet whether our apprehension of the "end and highest good" is itself
to be attributed to *phronēsis* has been the subject of lively scholarly
dispute. Under the influence of Julius Walter, E. Zeller denied that
the first principle or end of conduct is determined by *phronēsis*: "The
ultimate aims of action are determined, according to Aristotle, not by
deliberation but by the character of the will; or, as he would explain
it, while all aim at happiness, it depends upon the moral character
of each individual wherein he seeks it."[9]

A figure of considerable influence, Zeller, writes D. J. Allan,
brought Aristotle "into connection with Hume and with the modern
subjectivists and 'emotivists.'"[10] Yet our apprehension of "the ultimate
aims of action" need not be attributed to the appetitive faculty (*orexis*),
as if reason were merely "a slave of the passions," whose office is
but "to serve and obey them."[11] For, as Aristotle contends in Books
6 and 7 of the *Nicomachean Ethics* and in *De Anima* 3:7, the reflective
apprehension of "the good for oneself" is expressed in wish (*boulēsis*)
as the end (*telos*) or aim (*skopos*) of action.

Rational appetition (*boulēsis*) differs from *epithumia* (nonrational desire for the merely pleasant) and *thumos* (nonrational desire for objects under the appearance of the good), for "though what constitutes blessedness (*eudaimonia*) is utterly pleasant," in G. E. M. Anscombe's words, "it is not something one wants *because* it is a pleasure even though it should be no good." On the contrary, "it is the object of will as the *best* possible thing for a human being, being the activity of his rational part and the activity that is an end, not a means."[12]

For Aristotle, indeed, "blessedness" signifies the "most final" (*teleiotaton*) and "self-sufficient" (*autarkes*) of ends, in the sense that *eudaimonia* is sought merely for its own sake and, once attained, is perfectly fulfilling. The *eudaimōn* enjoys the good fully and without regret, so that if there is more than one activity fittingly described as an "end in itself," it will be included in *eudaimonia* as the end "final without qualification."

Interpreting *eudaimonia* in this fashion permits us to resolve the apparent fallacy of Nicomachean Ethics 1094a20, in which Aristotle assumes that since "we do not choose everything for the sake of something else (for this will involve an infinite progression)," there must be "*a* supreme good" as the *telos* of all purposive activity. For, as J. L. Ackrill observes, ends regarded as final in themselves may yet be "subordinate to one supreme end, *eudaimonia*," i.e., the predicate "most final" qualifies our "supreme good" as the set of activities themselves deemed "final."[13]

Saying that *eudaimonia* is one's "end and supreme good" is, as Aristotle says, a "truism" (*homologoumenon ti*) and in this respect not subject to deliberation.[14] In Anscombe's words, acceptance of the universal premise (that "such is the end and highest good") implies "intellectual acknowledgment of it as the guide to action," so that if an action is fittingly described as that which I have "best" reason to do, then I ought to perform it.[15] Were I to deliberate about whether I ought to do well, I would merely show that I am wanting the virtue of *phronēsis* as "reason which is with a view to something and is practical."[16]

Yet, as Aristotle hastens to observe, "a more distinctive account" of one's supreme end and highest good must be offered if the conclusion of practical reasoning is to result in choice (*prohairesis*) leading to action.[17] It is the burden of Aristotle's practical philosophy to show that *eudaimonia* is specified (semantically) by *aretē* as that which is "highest in the human being." For, as Anscombe remarks, attaining the "truth (*alētheia*) that corresponds to right appetition" in the "blessedness" of *eudaimonia* "is spoken of as the good working, or the work, of practical intelligence," since "desire must pursue the same things that the reasoning asserts."[18]

"Doing well" (*eupraxia*) is thus never a mere consequence of passion (*epithumia*), for rational appetition (*boulēsis*) is conceived "in terms of what is wanted being wanted *qua* conducive to or part of 'doing well,' or blessedness."[19] Were passion, indeed, merely an "original existence" implying "no reference to other passions," in Hume's words, it could not generate practical obligation.[20] As Bernard Williams argues apropos of Hume,

> [E]ven if we include all relevant statements about what we want; even if we include the general principles of decision theory that we are using (which must themselves be to some extent a matter of choice or temperament), it will still not be a matter of logical deduction to arrive at a conclusion about what we should do, all things considered.[21]

Obligation arises at some critical remove from the simple occurrence of desire (*epithumia*); and although "[o]n many occasions, it will be entirely obvious what is most important, and 'determining' will not require any episodic decision . . . there is still a step beyond the input." For it is always incumbent upon us to "determine what, on this particular occasion, in the light of everything, we judge most important."[22] Aristotle can thus deem the acts of the incontinent (*akratēs*) or licentious (*akolastos*) agent imprudent: the former inasmuch as desire frustrates action in accordance with one's rational wish (*boulēsis*), the latter inasmuch as desire (*orexis*) is itself misguided.

Regarding incontinent or licentious acts as "unreasonable" is not, as Hume assumes, "altogether inconceivable"; for *phronēsis* presumes our reflective apprehension (*hupolepsis*) of our "end and highest good." If, in Aristotle's words, "excellence in deliberation, *euboulia*, is one of the traits of persons of practical wisdom, we may regard this excellence as correct perception of that which conduces to the end, whereof *practical wisdom is a true judgment*."[23]

Aristotle's depiction of deliberation as "*pros to telos*" in Book 3 (1112b1) of the *Nicomachean Ethics* thus signifies not merely "means to an end" but "what is toward, or for the sake of the end." Such a construal is consistent with Aristotle's assertion that "virtue makes the aim right, while *phronēsis* ensures the correct means."[24] For moral virtue, in particular temperance (*sōphrosunē*), preserves a true belief concerning the good without implying that "virtue can, from its own resources, provide a conception of the good." Temperance, as Allan remarks, is "not an intellectual state, but a disposition towards pleasure and pain," and it is "by definition a 'right rule' imposed upon the passions, and can have no content prior to the ascertainment, by *phronēsis*, of this rule."[25]

Yet if the "ascertainment by *phronēsis*" of the right rule (*orthos logos*) is never reducible to *technē*, neither may it be merely assimilated to the theoretic model of demonstration (*apodeixis*). For unlike theoretical suppositions (in which cases are apodictically subsumed under universal rules), knowledge of the right rule implies *sōphrosunē*, since, for Aristotle, "it is from the repeated performance of just and temperate acts that we acquire virtues."[26] The judgments of *phronēsis* thus presuppose the acquisition of *aretē*:

> Syllogisms of action start from a judgment of the form "since such is the end and the highest good." Its nature need not here be specified. This premise does not appear at all except to the person of good character, for vice warps the judgment, and causes us to be deluded about the principles of action. From this it plainly follows that it is impossible to have practical wisdom without being a good person.[27]

Discernment of the virtuous mean presumes the "aesthetic" context of *phronēsis*, in which, through virtuous *paideia*, one cultivates the habits of loving and hating finely.[28] Experience (*empeiria*) illumines the context of acting, as the universal is reflectively apprehended in the "ultimate particularity" of action. Courage is thus relative to the "experience of particular kinds of risk" as it "is shown by different types of person in different kinds of danger."[29] Unlike deductive, theoretical inferences,

> matters concerned with conduct and questions of what is good for us have no fixity, any more than matters of health. The general account (of practical knowledge) being of this nature, the account of particular cases is yet more lacking in exactness; for they do not fall under any art or precept, but the agents

themselves in each case consider what is appropriate to the occasion.[30]

Since the virtuous mean "is relative to us," and hence to the context of its application, the virtuous agent (*spoudaios*) will have the proper feelings "at the right times on the right grounds towards the right people for the right motive and in the right way."[31] Yet "hitting the mark" with respect to the mean is by no means assured, for "questions of degree occur in particular cases, and the decision lies with our perception."[32]

The indefiniteness of the virtuous mean, as Vico observes, is thus not a limitation to be overcome, as if practical wisdom could aspire to Cartesian clarity and self-evidence by proceeding *more geometrico*. Recalling Aristotle's metaphor of the Lesbian metric, Vico writes, "It is therefore impossible to assess human affairs by the inflexible standard of abstract right; we must rather gauge them by the pliant Lesbic rule, which does not conform bodies to itself, but adjusts itself to their contours."[33] The "right rule" constituting the virtuous mean cannot be discerned in abstraction from the situation in which virtue is to be displayed. As Gadamer contends:

> The self-knowledge of which Aristotle speaks is characterized by the fact that it includes the perfect application and employs its knowledge in the immediacy of the given situation. Thus a knowledge of the particular situation (which is nevertheless not a perceptual seeing) is a necessary supplement to moral knowledge.[34]

Apprehension of the virtuous mean as a *universale concretum* is likened by Aristotle to a form of perception, though "not that of objects peculiar to one sense."[35] "Seeing" what is immediately to be done is ascribed to *nous*; for *nous* is

> concerned with judgments in both directions; because it is intuition [*nous*] and not reason that grasps both the first and the ultimate terms: the intuition concerned with demonstration having as its objects the primary immutable terms, and the intuition that operates in practical inferences being concerned with the ultimate and contingent, i.e., the minor premise. For these are the starting-points for arriving at the end, because it is from

particular instances that general rules are established. So these particulars need to be perceived; and this perception is intuition.[36]

The perception (*aisthēsis*) of the ultimate particular thus generates a description of action that specifies one's "end and highest good." The action is *ultimate*, that is, inasmuch as it is apprehended as an end in itself, expressing "knowledge of the good for myself." Yet inasmuch as this knowledge is mediated in the ultimate *particularity* of *praxis* (as the conclusion of one's deliberation), it is, as David Wiggins remarks, "the subject matter of the minor premise" which finally exhibits one's "understanding of the reason for performing an action, or its end." For "the major premise and the generalizable concern that comes with it arise from this perception of something particular."[37]

For Aristotle, "practical reasonableness, *phronēsis*, as well as theoretical reasonableness (*sophia*) are 'bestnesses' (*aretai*)," i.e., that "which is highest in the human being—what Aristotle likes to call '*nous*' or the divine."[38] Our perfection reflects our finite, eidetic determination (*ti estin*): our blessedness (*eudaimonia*), inclusive "of all intrinsic goods," is conceived architectonically, as an end "final without qualification," constitutively specified by the moral, no less than the intellectual, virtues.[39]

THE VIRTUES AS EXCELLENCES (ARETAI) OF THE PERFECT COMMUNITY

In modern analytical terms, one might say that the reflective apperception (*aisthēsis*) of the ultimate particular generates a "semantically opaque" context inasmuch as actions are fittingly described in terms of one's "knowledge of the good for oneself." Attaining practical "truth" signifies the occurrence not merely an "original" event (to which one refers in rationalizations) but of *eupraxia* (doing well) as the consequence of "right appetition." While this "quasi-intensional" aspect of action descriptions will further occupy us in chapter 5, it suffices for the moment to observe that the description of *aretē*, which in Anscombe's words is "made true" in acting, cannot be abstracted from the "aesthetic" context of the *phronimos's* "self-knowledge."[40]

In Aristotle's terms, the notion of *eupraxia* implies a distinction of virtuous actions as exhibiting "a certain quality" from the further determination of such actions as done from "a certain state."[41] Socrates acts courageously when his action is in conformity with the right rule (*orthos logos*) of *aretē* and when his action, so defined, is intended *per se*, for "its own sake, from a fixed and permanent disposition."[42] Virtuous actions "imply" the right rule, and must be distinguished from actions merely in conformity with the right rule, intended *per accidens*, as a means, for instance, of attaining pleasure.[43]

Actions intended as specifications of *eudaimonia per se* exhibit the "that" (*hoti*) of an action in terms of its "because" (*dioti*), so that, fully explicated, "Socrates acted courageously" implies that Socrates performed an action displaying the relevant "qualities" in "a courageous way," i.e., from the requisite intentional "state." The sense of "courage" for Socrates could not, then, be grasped in abstraction from its "aesthetic," evaluative signification. "How we 'go on' from one application of a concept to another," writes Bernard Williams, "is a function of the kind of interest that the concept represents, and we should not assume that we could see how people 'go on' if we did not share the evaluative perspective in which this kind of concept has its point."[44] Even in imaginatively "anticipating the use of the concept," one must "grasp imaginatively its evaluative point."[45]

The twin Apollonian precepts of the virtuous mean (*mēden agan*) and knowledge of oneself (*gnōthi seauton*) are thus brought into a reflective harmony of what Aristotle terms "self-knowledge."[46] Expressing the connaturality of *aretē*, the self-knowledge of the *phronimos* is not that of an abstract *res cogitans*, for it is not finally one thing for Socrates to be Socrates and yet another for Socrates to be virtuous. As Stuart Hampshire observes, within Aristotelian ethical theory there is "no ultimate divergence in the normal run of things between a morally admirable life and a satisfying and happy one, for to the man who is rational in substantial practical matters it has become *second nature* to act rightly and he does so more or less effortlessly and as a matter of course and with pleasure."[47]

The reflective dialectic of "self-knowledge" and *aretē* implies that only intensionally equivalent redescriptions of virtue, reflecting Socrates' reasons, would satisfy the expression "Socrates performed the courageous action intentionally." The sense of Socrates's courageous action will be relative to Socrates's intention to act "as a courageous person would act." The description of courageous action "implies" the right rule in its rationalization, for, although pleasure attends virtuous actions, Socrates's delight in fine actions is epiphenomenal to their being fine.[48]

Socrates's "knowledge of the good" must accordingly be distinguished from hedonistic or egoistic theories of motivation; for the formal (syntactical) requirement of acting in accordance with one's "end and supreme good" does not permit the (semantical) inference of acting from "rational self-love." (In chapter 5, we will consider whether there are formal limits to a theory of the good, but for the present, we might simply observe that such a theory is not given *a limine* as hedonistic or egoistic.)

In specifying what is best for a human being, the Aristotelian doctrine of *eudaimonia* does not propose perfection as itself a *further* reason or motive for acting, as if virtuous action were done for the sake of self-love. As modern utilitarians are wont to observe, such "perfectionism" might well seem "morally self-indulgent."[49] Yet for the Aristotelian *phronimos*, virtuous action is done "for the sake of *eudaimonia*" without thereby implying that it is "a means to producing something other than itself."[50] For only if the *phronimos's* self-knowledge is "at the same time . . . expressive of [his virtuous dispositions]" would his moral perfection be "final without qualification."[51]

Socrates's virtuous dispositions are thus not self-regarding in the morally onerous sense of the term. For not only is the idea of perfection tempered by "particular justice"; it has as its natural harmonic the ideal fruition of the common good in the formation of the just *polis*. "General justice" is "complete virtue in the fullest sense" precisely as it "tends to produce or conserve the happiness (and the constituents of the happiness) of a political association," to which are subordinated all domestic and merely individual goods.[52] In attaining "general justice," as Theognis (or Phocylides) says, "the whole of virtue is summed up."[53]

For Aristotle, the virtuous life unfolds against the rich tapestry of the *polis*; here its gestures are charged with significance and derive their characteristic form and force. The life of virtue presupposes the *polis*, even as the end of the *polis* is the perfection of the citizen (*polites*) through education and training in virtue (*paideia*). "A *polis*," writes Aristotle, "is constituted by the association of families and villages in a *perfect* and self-sufficing existence; and such an existence . . . consists in a life of true felicity and goodness [for the *polites*]."[54]

For Thomas Aquinas, a faithful disciple of Aristotle in this respect, moral perfection presumes the "*communitas perfecta*" as the "common good is the end or purpose of individual persons living in the community."[55] General justice, or "*justitia legalis*," is accorded primacy over all the moral virtues inasmuch as it directs them to the "common good," which "surpasses the individual good of one person."[56] For it is only when regarded in light of "general justice" as "complete virtue in *the fullest sense*" that the *aretai* satisfy the formal definition of *eudaimonia* (as "final" and "self-sufficient"). The reflective judgments of the *phronimos* imply, then, a common perception of "sublimity," a common "seeking what is right" (*sunesis*), even as the sublimity of the perfect community (*koinōnia teleios*) is expressed in the blessedness (*eudaimonia*) of its members: in the sublimity of the perfect community, all share singly, not en masse.[57]

The "right (universal) rule" of the virtuous mean is thus not excogitated "independently of all experience," as Kant supposed. On the contrary, the *aretai* express the rich heritage of a linguistic community likened by Burke to a "bank and capital of the ages," which grows "by a gradual process of social accumulation and transmission."[58] For, unlike the rules of mathematics or physics, the right rule of *aretē*, considered in abstraction from the virtuous community, possesses a merely schematic significance. Indeed, the practical instantiation of the universal (through the reflective judgments which give it force) represents not a diminishment but an "accretion of reality" of the rule itself.[59]

Thus the "sophistic puzzle" that it is not finally "possible to be good in the true sense of the word without prudence, or to be prudent without moral goodness" is resolved.[60] For the "moral goodness" or "sublimity" of the virtuous community is presupposed by the *phronimos*, even as the reflective judgments of the *phronimos* "make true" moral goodness or fineness of character. In the common knowledge and *praxis* of *aretē*, the *phronimos* comes to "self-knowledge" as his character (*ēthos*) is formed through habituation (*ethismos*), his sharing in what Heraclitus called "the common" (*xynon*).

NOTES TO CHAPTER 1

1. Sophocles *Antigone*, line 1049, p. 154.
2. Plato *Theaetetus* 167c.
3. Hans-Georg Gadamer, *The Idea of the Good in Platonic-Aristotelian Philosophy*, trans. P. Christopher Smith (New Haven: Yale University Press, 1986), 171.
4. Aristotle *Nicomachean Ethics* 1142a23–29. Unless otherwise noted, the translation is that of J. A. K. Thomson, as revised by Hugh Tredennick (Harmondsworth, England: Penguin Books, 1976).

5. Ibid., 1140a24–b10.

6. Ibid., 1141b33, 1142a30; *Aristotle's Eudemian Ethics* 1246b36.

7. Cf. Hans-Georg Gadamer, *Truth and Method*, trans. Joel Weinsheimer and Donald G. Marshall, 2nd ed. (New York: Crossroad, 1991), 316; *The Idea of the Good*, 177.

8. Aristotle *Nicomachean Ethics* 1144a23–36.

9. Eduard Zeller, *Aristotle and the Earlier Peripatetics*, trans. B. F. C. Costelloe and J. H. Muirhead, vol. 2 (New York: Russell and Russell, 1962), 182–83.

10. D. J. Allan, "Aristotle's Account of the Origin of Moral Principles," in *Articles on Aristotle: Ethics and Politics*, ed. Jonathan Barnes, Malcolm Schofield, and Richard Sorabji (New York: St. Martin's Press, 1978), 74.

11. David Hume, *A Treatise of Human Nature*, in vol. 2 of *British Moralists, 1650–1800*, ed. D. D. Raphael (Oxford: Clarendon Press, 1969), 2:(482), 5.

12. G. E. M. Anscombe, "Thought and Action in Aristotle," in *Articles on Aristotle: Ethics and Politics*, 69 (emphasis added).

13. J. L. Ackrill, "Aristotle on *Eudaimonia*," in *Essays on Aristotle's Ethics*, ed. Amélie Oksenberg Rorty (Berkeley: University of California Press, 1980), 23–24.

14. Aristotle *Nicomachean Ethics* 1097b22.

15. Anscombe, "Thought and Action in Aristotle," 69.

16. Aristotle *Nicomachean Ethics* 1139a36 (the translation is by Anscombe, in "Thought and Action in Aristotle," 69).

17. Ibid., 1097b22.

18. Anscombe, "Thought and Action in Aristotle," 70–71; Aristotle *Nicomachean Ethics* 1139a21–30.

19. Anscombe, "Thought and Action in Aristotle," 69.

20. Hume, *A Treatise of Human Nature*, (490, 504), 9, 19.

21. Bernard Williams, *Ethics and the Limits of Philosophy* (Cambridge: Harvard University Press, 1985), 126.

22. Ibid.

23. Aristotle *Nicomachean Ethics* 1142b31–33 (the translation is by David Wiggins, "Deliberation and Practical Reason," in *Essays on Aristotle's Ethics*, 230 [emphasis added]). Cf. *Nicomachean Ethics* 1139a21 and 1152b1.

24. Aristotle *Nicomachean Ethics* 1144a6.

25. Allan, "Aristotle's Account of the Origin of Moral Principles," 77.

26. Aristotle *Nicomachean Ethics* 1105b10.

27. Ibid., 1144a23 (the translation is by Allan, in "Aristotle's Account of the Origin of Moral Principles," 77).

28. Ibid., 1179b24

29. Ibid., 1116b3.

30. Ibid., 1104a7 (the translation is by Wiggins, in "Deliberation and Practical Reason," 231). Cf. 1107a28.

31. Ibid., 1106b21.

32. Ibid., 1109b21–26.

33. Giambattista Vico, *On the Study Methods of Our Time*, trans. Elio Gianturco (Indianapolis: Bobbs-Merrill, 1965), 34.

34. Gadamer, *Truth and Method*, 322.

35. Aristotle *Nicomachean Ethics* 1142a29.

36. Ibid., 1143a36–b5.

37. Wiggins, "Deliberation and Practical Reason," 236.

38. Gadamer, *The Idea of the Good*, 175. See Aristotle *Nicomachean Ethics* 1139b2.

39. Aristotle *Nicomachean Ethics* 1097a30.

40. Anscombe, "Thought and Action in Aristotle," 71. See Donald Davidson, *Essays on Actions and Events* (Oxford: Clarendon Press, 1980), 5.

41. Aristotle *Nicomachean Ethics* 1105a30.

42. Ibid.

43. Ibid., 1144b20.

44. Williams, *Ethics and the Limits of Philosophy*, 141.

45. Ibid., 142.

46. Aristotle *Nicomachean Ethics* 1141b33. See Gadamer, *Truth and Method*, 316.

47. Stuart Hampshire, "Public and Private Morality," in *Public and Private Morality*, ed. Stuart Hampshire (Cambridge: Cambridge University Press, 1978), 28 (emphasis added).

48. Aristotle *Nicomachean Ethics* 1144b20.

49. See the discussion in Bernard Williams, *Moral Luck: Philosophical Papers, 1973–1980* (Cambridge: Cambridge University Press, 1981), 40–53.

50. Aristotle *Nicomachean Ethics* 1039a30.

51. Bernard Williams, *Ethics and the Limits of Philosophy*, 51.

52. Aristotle *Nicomachean Ethics* 1129b6–1130b8. Cf. 1141b24; *Politics* 1252a25–1253a38.

53. Aristotle *Nicomachean Ethics* 1129b30.

54. Aristotle *Politics*, trans. Ernest Barker (London: Oxford University Press, 1946), 1280b32–1281a10 (emphasis added). The Aristotelian conception of the "perfect community" reflects its finality and sufficiency for human flourishing. See *Nicomachean Ethics* 1094b7–10, 1129b15, 1160a9; *Politics* 1252a1–1253a38. Cf. also the commentary of Thomas Aquinas in *Summa Theologiae* I-II, Q. 90, a. 2. The translation is by Thomas Gilby (New York: McGraw Hill, 1964–81).

55. Aquinas, *Summa Theologiae* II-II, Q. 58, a. 7, 9.

56. Ibid., Q. 58, a. 6, 12.

57. Aristotle *Nicomachean Ethics* 1094b7–10 (emphasis added).

58. Edmund Burke, *Reflections on the Revolution in France and on the Proceedings in Certain Societies in London Relative to That Event*, in Ernest Barker, translator's introduction to *Natural Law and the Theory of Society* by Otto Gierke (Cambridge: Cambridge University Press, 1958), xlix.

59. Gadamer, *The Idea of the Good*, 164–65; *Truth and Method*, 320–24.

60. Aristotle *Nicomachean Ethics* 1144b31. Cf. 1105a17–20, and *Metaphysics* 9.8.

2

The Kantian Crucible

"Duty! Thou sublime and mighty name that dost embrace nothing charming or insinuating but requirest submission . . . what origin is there worthy of thee, and where is to be found the root of thy noble descent which proudly rejects all kinship with the inclinations and from which to be descended is the indispensable condition of the only worth which men can give themselves?"[1]

IMMANUEL KANT

If, like Eliot's Magi, we behold the sublime revelation of duty, like them we may wonder whether it is a birth or a death we witness.[2] For the rich heritage of Aristotelian *phronēsis* was not fated to endure. The eclipse of the classical ethical ideal of practical wisdom heralded the rise of a "new philosophy," in which ethics ceased to rest in the virtuous habituation of character (*ēthos*). Having its "seat and origin in reason completely a priori," Morality must slouch towards Königsberg to be born.[3]

Yet, as Valéry might say, the Aristotelian doctrine of *aretē* was not so much refuted as abandoned in modernity. If in Aristotelian *eudaimonia* "Felicity of this life, consisteth . . . in the repose of a mind satisfied," it is precisely the want of this which impresses Hobbes. For "there is no such *Finis ultimus*, (utmost ayme,) nor *Summum Bonum*, (greatest Good)." Felicity "is the continuall progresse of the desire, from one object to another; the attaining of the former, being still but the way to the latter."[4]

Construing felicity in terms amenable to empirical methodology, Hobbes assumes that the victorious desire terminating deliberation (as the transmission of motions) explains the transmission of practical obligation.[5] With the attenuation of *boulēsis* to mere appetite (*epithumia*), prudence is reduced to technical expertise. Reason is but the servant of interest as "the Thoughts, are to the Desires, as Scouts and Spies, to range abroad, and find the way to the things Desired."[6]

"Prudent" thus becomes a commendation of Hume's "sensible knave," whose cleverness is devoted to the pursuit of "self-love and private interest."[7] For if the realm of value emerges as a purely subjective constitution explicable in terms of the mere incidence of pain or pleasure, then, as Hume says, there can be "no eternal rational measures of right and wrong."[8] In the *Treatise* Hume writes, "If given a reason, therefore, for the pleasure or uneasiness [experienced], we sufficiently explain the vice or virtue."[9] And yet the notion of interest retains a certain, beneficent ambiguity for Hume.

In the *Inquiry* Hume recognizes that obligation arises not from the mere intensity of the passions but rather from the "social sympathy in human nature," expressed in the "sentiment of humanity," "common to all mankind," since the "humanity of one man is the humanity of everyone."[10] The "natural pleasures" attending the virtuous life are "really without price." For "there is not, in any instance, the smallest pretext for giving [vice] the preference above virtue with a view to self-interest."[11] Our "sentiments of humanity and sympathy" inspire "moral approbation" and hence "moral obligation," so that prudential judgment presumes a right appetition, corresponding to "the best possible thing for a human being."[12]

Ariel-like in their manifestation, the "natural" sentiments satisfying prudence recall the Aristotelian conception of rational wish (*boulēsis*), irreducible to a positivist construal of passion. Yet the Humean legacy rendered such a prudential account of virtue increasingly untenable. In opposing Hume, Kant depicts reverence for humanity as the issue of aprioristic legislation, while viewing happiness as the hedonistic pursuit of rational self-love. No feat of conceptual legerdemain conjures moral virtue from prudential regard for one's "dear self": henceforth, it is prudence that must be "limited" and "controlled."[13]

In the first section we consider the technical reduction of Aristotelian *phronēsis* as a prelude to a critical assessment of Kantian *Moralität*. In the second section I argue that the distinction of hypothetical (prudential) and categorical imperatives is finally one of modality rather than of logical form. Yet the modal distinction raises further questions, for, as I contend in the third and fourth sections respectively, Kant fails to show the practical necessity and sufficiency of universal prescription for the generation of moral maxims. Indeed, as I argue in Part Two, Kant's modern heirs redress the lacunae of *Moralität* by imposing the formal constraints of universality upon hypothetical (prudential) imperatives.

THE TECHNICAL REDUCTION OF PRUDENCE

Spun of abstract reflection, virtue, for Kant, is no longer the internal fruition of *phronēsis* but a rein upon it as the "subjective principle of self-love."[14] The perfection of prudence (*Klugheit*) is not "practical wisdom" in the service of the perfect community but, rather, "personal wisdom" (*Privatklugheit*), which Kant defines as "sagacity in combining all [one's] ends to [one's] own lasting advantage."[15] "Prudence" suffers a sea change as the "boundaries between [prudential] self-love and morality" become "distinct and sharp."[16]

Denial of the First Thesis (That the Phronimos Intends Virtuous Activity for Its Own Sake)

In Kantian *Moralität*, the apodictic force of moral prescription derives from the "mere Idea of the qualification of a maxim for the universality of a practical law."[17] Only a categorically prescribed action is "good *in itself* and therefore . . . necessary, in virtue of its principle, for a will which of itself accords with reason."[18] For only such "dutiful" actions can be conceived as intrinsic goods of the agent, regarded under the aspect of "our proper self" as "*homo noumenon*."[19]

Aristotelian eudaimonism becomes, for Kant, a form of *poiēsis* ordered to the "producible ends" of pleasure. Yet his assumption that if "the action would be good solely as a means *to something else*, the imperative is hypothetical" is unduly restrictive. For, as we have seen, the end of an action hypothetically prescribed need not be a producible state of affairs distinct from the action itself.[20] Virtuous action (*eupraxia*), for Aristotle, is not merely a means to doing well but, rather, specifically constitutes blessedness (as "what is best for a human being").

Kant errs, then, in regarding Aristotelian virtue as a mere means to the ulterior end of pleasure. And yet, as Anscombe observes, even actions regarded as mere means would be apodictically necessary if it can be shown that they are the only or the best means to attaining the proposed end (and if the end is itself consistent with, or constitutive of, one's supreme good).[21] A fortiori, virtuous action, in Aristotle's sense of the term, would be "necessary in virtue of its principle," i.e., as a specification of one's end and supreme good, even if not derived from the mere idea of a "will which of itself conforms to reason."[22]

Kant, indeed, appears to admit as much in his analysis of hypothetical imperatives, which, expressing "an *objective* law of reason," are practically "necessitating" for imperfect rational agents. Explicating the practically rational sense of "ought" (*Sollen*), Kant distinguishes hypothetical imperatives of skill (obtaining with problematic modal force "if" I will the end) and hypothetical imperatives of prudence (obtaining with assertoric force "since" I will the end). The formal principle of hypothetical imperatives, whether problematic or assertoric, expresses the "analytical truth" that "if or since I will the end, I also will the action required for it."[23] The import of this analytical truth in the practical realm is such that I act irrationally if, willing an end, I fail to adopt the requisite means to attain it.

Categorical imperatives, conversely, obtain with apodictic modal force, expressing the purely formal principle that one "[a]ct only on that maxim through which you can at the same time will that it should become a universal law."[24] It is incumbent upon Kant, then, to distinguish the "objective necessity" attending every well-formed practical prescription (whether hypothetical or categorical) from the subset of well-formed practical prescriptions comprising categorical (apodictic) imperatives. For, consistent with the tenor of his own analysis, prudential imperatives ordered to my end and highest good will be "objectively necessary," and hence practically "necessitating," even if the scope of the universal "right rule" of virtue is restricted to the domain of the virtuous community. While Kant, for instance, would describe Antigone's burying of the slain Polynices as a "production" serving an ulterior end, Aristotle might respond that her action is only *per accidens* a production (*poiēsis*), for *per se*, her action represents a rendering of filial obligation. Formal, final, and efficient causes coalesce in the generation of an action description, i.e., her fulfilling the "unwritten, unalterable laws of God and heaven."[25] Sophocles depicts Antigone as desiring her obsequies "for their own sake," so specifying her "blessedness," and not merely as means to a producible end. Her action would thus be "objectively necessary" (even if not "objectively necessary in itself without reference to some purpose").[26]

Denial of the Second Thesis (That the Virtues Are Excellences of the Perfect Community)

The Kantian reduction of Aristotelian *aretē* to *technē* is reminiscent of the Sophists' in yet another respect; for his empirical psychology is hedonistic. Kantian morality is decidedly postlapsarian; one assumes that moral precepts are neither congenial nor connatural to our wayward natures. "Virtues," as Eliot says, "are forced upon us by our impudent crimes."[27]

In his critique of Wolff and his scholastic forebears, Kant denies the moral relevance of the distinction of the higher and lower faculties of desire (the *appetitus rationalis* and *appetitus sensitivus*). "All material practical principles," writes Kant, "are, as such, of one and the same kind, and belong under the general principle of self-love or one's own happiness."[28] As this passage suggests, Kant's hedonistic psychology is at once egoistic: "[T]o seek happiness and to seek one's own happiness," writes Beck, "are tacitly identified."[29] In the "Analytic of Empirical Practical Reason" prudence is thus conceived as generating *singular* imperatives, devoted to one's own "selfish" interests, while in the *Groundwork* Kant sharply delineates the "practically good . . . which determines the will by concepts of reason" from "the pleasant . . . which influences the will, not as a principle of reason valid for everyone, but solely through the medium of sensation by purely subjective causes valid only for the senses of this person or that."[30]

Yet, as we have seen, Kant's depiction of prudence as "rational self-love" in the pursuit of pleasure "valid only for . . . this person or that" betrays a confusion of the semantics of practical judgment (synthetically elaborated in an empirical theory of hedonistic motivation) with the objective (analytical) law of reason comprising the formal principle of prudential (assertoric) imperatives.[31] For the formal requirement that I act in accordance with *my* highest end or supreme good does not imply that my reasons be hedonistic or egoistic, i.e., that my happiness be conceived independently of the "common felicity." For Aristotle and Aquinas, indeed, the "final end" of prudence *is* the common good, so that the "right rule" of *aretē* obtains with *universal* prescriptive force for the virtuous community. The virtuous mean (*mēden agan*) is not a counsel of pleasure, "valid only for . . . this person or that," but a rule expressing our common perception of excellence.[32]

The Limits of Prudential Imperatives

Kant's mistaken belief that only a categorically prescribed action is "objectively necessary in itself without reference to . . . any further end" is abetted by the semantical indefiniteness of his notion of happiness.[33] For prudential actions, as we have seen, can be objectively prescribed only if they can be conceived as constitutive specifications of happiness or as necessary means to its attainment. Yet if the conception of happiness bears no definite reference, no "objectively necessary" action can be prescribed in the apodosis of the imperative.

Hypothetical (assertoric) imperatives of prudence prescribe that one act in accordance with one's "own greatest well-being," which Kant conceives as "a purpose which we can presuppose a priori and with certainty to be present in every man because it belongs to his very being."[34] As an ideal of the imagination, happiness implies "an absolute whole, a maximum of well-being in my present, and in every future state."[35] Yet the cognitive content of my own "greatest well-being," the constituents of which are "without exception empirical," is so obscure that Kant concludes:

> If it were only as easy to find a determinate concept of happiness [as the merely possible purposes of problematic imperatives], the imperatives of prudence would agree entirely with those of skill and *would be equally analytic*. For here as there it could alike be said "Who wills the end, wills also (necessarily if he accords with reason) the sole means which are in his power." Unfortunately, however, the concept of happiness is so indeterminate a concept that although every man wants to attain happiness, he can never say definitely and in unison with himself what it really is that he wants and wills.[36]

Lacking such omniscience, "we cannot act on determinate principles in order to be happy, but only on empirical counsels."[37] For Kant, indeed, "imperatives of prudence, speaking strictly, do not command at all—that is, cannot exhibit actions objectively as practically necessary," and hence "they are rather to be taken as recommendations (*consilia*), than as commands (*praecepta*), of reason."[38] "The maxim of self-love (prudence) merely advises; the law of morality commands."[39]

Yet the inference that "there is no imperative possible which in the strictest sense could command us to do what will make us happy" is consequent upon the *synthetic* (semantical) indeterminacy of Kant's conception of happiness; the imperative of prudence has not ceased to be, in Kant's own terms, "an analytic practical proposition."[40] As H. J. Paton remarks, the formal principle "remains analytic however many synthetic propositions may be required in order to determine theoretically the means to our happiness."[41] As in the case of hypothetical imperatives of skill, the formal requirement of the intentional coherence of "willing the end" and "willing the necessary means (in one's power)" is logically prior to the determination of the cognitive content of one's end. In his distinction between the two imperatives, Kant errs, writes Beck, for " '[i]n what concerns the will,' both are analytical . . . ; in what concerns the understanding, i.e., the cognitive content in the choice of particular means to the end in view, both are synthetic."[42]

Prudential imperatives differ from technical imperatives in that prudence introduces the idea of a "total" or comprehensive end in the specification of one's "greatest well-being" or "lasting advantage." For the concept of happiness implies "that any rational agent who wills a total end will necessarily—so far as reason has a decisive influence over his actions—will the constituents of that end as well as the means to it."[43] Since "this proposition would be merely analytic" (and hence independent of Kant's hedonistic premises), its practical relevance is displayed not in the derivation of discrete ends but in their evaluative comparison: in the practical requirement, that is, that I act not only intentionally but in accordance with what I have "greatest" reason to do.[44]

Although explicit only in Kant's later writings, this inclusive function of "happiness" recalls the Aristotelian conception of an end "final without qualification." (The synthetic indeterminacy of "happiness," indeed, presumes the force of this practical requirement, for only if one conceives happiness as "an absolute whole, a maximum of well-being in my present, and in every future state" does its interpretation pose a problem for practical reason.)[45]

The Limits of Technical Imperatives

With the attenuation of the force of prudential imperatives to mere *consilia*, the technical reduction of *phronēsis* is complete. For, unlike prudential imperatives, technical imperatives "exhibit [the agent's] actions objectively as practically *necessary*." Yet even here perplexities arise, for it is by no means perspicuous that the general formula of technical (problematic) imperatives suffices for the objective determination of action. Since technical imperatives do not justify an action *per se*, but only relative to a contingent, "merely possible purpose," my intention to perform an action would be justified even though my end failed to enjoy deliberative priority.[46] As Alan Donagan observes, such technical imperatives do "not prescribe that you are to do what you most want to do, whether you are to achieve the end proposed, or to abstain from the only effective means of achieving it."[47] As the modal conclusion "one ought to perform 'A' under the description 'd'" is detached from the ensemble of beliefs and attitudes comprising one's best reason(s) for acting, even the incontinent agent might be said to deliberate in this "technical" sense.

Just as the semantic indefiniteness of Kant's notion of happiness fails to justify an objective, prudential determination of action, so the indeterminacy of one's ends (with respect to one's best reasons) in technical reasoning precludes our describing an action as an *"ultimate particular."* For it is consistent with the restrictive scope of technical reasoning in its Kantian construal that I ought to perform action 'A' under one description yet ought to refrain from performing 'A' under another. After all, there is nothing inconsistent about the attribution of implicitly conflicting desires. Like Catullus, it may be that

I hate and I love. And if you ask me how,
I do not know: I only feel it, and I'm torn in two.[48]

A mere recitation of desires as possible, prima facie reasons implied in alternative action descriptions fails to resolve Catullus's dilemma.

Were Kant merely too sanguine in his belief that "there is no difficulty in regard to the possibility of [hypothetical imperatives]," a reformulation of the Kantian doctrine of prudence would be unproblematic.[49] Yet the difficulty lies elsewhere, for so long as the traditional tenets of morality fail to admit of a *prudential* justification, a distinctively "moral" foundation of virtue commends itself. (Such, indeed, seems the burden of the "analytical" methodology of chapters 1 and 2 of the *Groundwork*, in which Kant argues regressively "from common [moral] knowledge to the formation of its supreme principle.")[50]

Once, however, we concede that the Aristotelian *phronimos* intends virtue for its own sake as a "common excellence" of the perfect community, the a priori opposition of prudence and our common (moral) knowledge becomes chimerical. For the *phronimos*, no less than the Kantian moral agent, is concerned "with the rationality or goodness of the end" and not merely with "what must be done to attain it."[51] Virtuous action, intended for its own sake, is "objectively necessary" even prior to our "passage to a critique of pure practical reason."[52]

THE DISTINCTION OF HYPOTHETICAL AND CATEGORICAL IMPERATIVES

Kant might, nonetheless, object that our account of common moral knowledge, restricted as it is to the domain of the virtuous community, remains "contingent and precarious." For the virtues of the Aristotelian *phronimos* would be but "vain illusion and splendid misery" if they fail to partake of "the moral law in its purity and genuineness," which "is to be looked for nowhere else than in a pure philosophy."[53] Only thus, for Kant, can morality escape the spectre of sophistic relativism.

So our attention turns to Kant's account of morality and his distinction of hypothetical and categorical imperatives. "A categorical imperative," writes Kant, "would be one which represented an action as objectively necessary in itself apart from its relation to a further end."[54] Yet the ostensible grammatical distinction of hypothetical and categorical imperatives is belied by Kant's own analysis. For the mere absence of allusion to subjective ends need not imply the "objective necessity" of an action. As Philippa Foot observes, manners imitate morals in this respect, since "behaviour is required not simply recommended."[55] Kant himself acknowledges that an imperative that "appears to be categorical and unconditioned" (with respect to its grammatical form) may "in fact be only a pragmatic prescription calling attention to our advantage and merely bidding us take this into account."[56] Conversely, moral imperatives may themselves be expressed in hypothetical form, as in the locution "If you have promised to do such and such, then you must do it."[57]

The Logical Distinction

One wonders, then, if the pertinent difference is one of logical form, i.e., if there is a distinctive moral sense of "ought" (*Sollen*). If one assumes that the fact that I ought to perform 'A' is a reason for my performing 'A', the sense of the "moral 'should'" would, in Foot's words, "be relevantly different from the 'shoulds' appearing in normative statements of other kinds."[58] Kant's assertion that moral action is done solely "for the sake of duty" might then be construed in terms of what Bernard Williams refers to as the "Kantian Requirement" that one ought (morally) to act "from a specific motive, namely from the thought that [one] ought" so to act.[59]

In such a construal, the logical form of moral prescription would no longer be represented in terms of the propositional operator 'O(p)' (i.e., it ought to be the case "that 'p'") where 'p' signifies the state of affairs represented by one's intentionally doing such and such.[60] For the action description signified by 'p' would imply the thought that 'O(p)'. "If the Kantian Requirement holds," writes Williams, "then we cannot determinately specify in such a case what state of affairs it is that ought to come about, since the agent's thought has to be part of that state of affairs, and when we come to specify that thought, the question arises again, and we are involved in an unavoidable regress or indeterminacy."[61] The concept of duty would be no less indefinite than that of happiness. As Sir David Ross has argued, if Kant defines "It is my duty to act A" as "It is my duty to act A from the sense that it is my duty to act A," duty is defined in terms of itself.[62]

Yet there is reason to believe that Kant has not defined duty in such regressive terms. "Kant is merely showing," writes Stephan Körner, "that in using the notion of duty, even before philosophizing about it, we often distinguish between actions which externally conform to duty (*pflichtmässige Handlungen*) and actions done for the sake of or from duty (*Handlungen aus Pflicht*)."[63] Action is "dutiful" in the latter sense precisely inasmuch as it exhibits our "interest in the action itself and in its rational principle (namely, the law)."[64]

The logical function of "dutiful" rests, then, not in specifying a further reason for acting, but rather in showing that one's intention to act in accordance with the pure, universal form of law is decisive, i.e., that no "further reason" is necessary.[65] Actions are thus justified not merely in virtue of their extrinsic "regulative" conformity with universal law but, rather, precisely *because* their maxims exhibit this conformity. Maxims, reflecting the "rational principle (namely, the law)" function "constitutively" in justifying action, for our "interest in the action itself" is governed by the formal universality of its maxim.[66]

Inasmuch as the property of universality may be attributed to maxims (and hence indirectly to the actions they govern), it may be conceived as a relevant "desirability characteristic" of the action signified in 'p', specifiable independently of the thought that 'O(p)'.[67] To act "dutifully" expresses one's intention to perform the action signified in 'p' "for the sake" of the regulative conformity of its maxim with universal (moral) law. Actions done for the sake of duty (*Handlungen aus Pflicht*, signified in 'p'), would thus fall within the scope of what I "ought" to do ('O(p)').

As Aristotle distinguishes the "quality" of acting (e.g., conformity with the "right rule" of courage) from the "state" of the agent (one's acting *as* a courageous agent, who intends virtuous *praxis per se*), so Kant distinguishes actions conforming to duty from actions done "for the sake of duty." Virtue is intended "for its own sake," albeit, for Kant, the pertinent quality of action is already a possible intentional state, i.e., one's maxim regarded as a potential reason for acting.[68] An action (e.g., promise keeping) whose maxims exhibit a "fitness" for universal law is intended "for the sake" of this universality.

From the perspective of Kantian *Moralität*, an action is justified only insofar as "the will is determined solely by the law *without any further motive.*"[69] Fitness of one's maxims for universal law would thus constitute one's *best* reason or motive for acting. One prescribes objectively inasmuch as one intends that possible (subjective) maxims be conformed to the pure form of law expressed in the categorical imperative that one "[a]ct only on that maxim through which you can at the same time will that it should become a universal law."[70]

The Modal Distinction

If we suppose that a "purely good will" for Kant is one whose best reasons are determined by the pure, universal form of law, "ought" (*Sollen*) would govern "dutiful actions" (*Handlungen aus*

Pflicht) without regressively comprising a "further motive" for acting. My dutiful actions would form a subset of the actions I ought to perform (since "all imperatives are expressed by an 'ought'").[71] As Kant himself admits, "dutiful" actions and actions that I "ought" to perform differ logically in extension, for the actions of a perfectly rational agent would be dutiful but not subject to practical prescription:

> A perfectly good will would thus stand quite as much under objective laws (laws of the good), but it could not on this account be conceived as *necessitated* to act in conformity with law, since of itself, in accordance with its subjective constitution, it can be determined only by the concept of the good. Hence for the *divine* will, and in general for a *holy* will, there are no imperatives: "*I ought*" is here out of place, because "*I will*" is already of itself in harmony with the law.[72]

One must accordingly distinguish (i) the formal universality of the "objective *law*," characterizing all well-formed practical prescriptions of the form 'O(p)', i.e., that a rational agent will act in accordance with her best reason(s), all things considered, and ought to do so if tempted otherwise, from (ii) "the *moral* law," which specifies (semantically) what I "ought" to do (in the interpretation of the intentional action description signified in 'p'). Rather than generating a distinct logical syntax of "ought," the moral law would thus serve as a semantical rule for the interpretation of my best reason(s).

For Kant, the supreme moral law is distinguished from other possible semantical rules, such as the "right rule" of *aretē* of the Aristotelian *phronimos*, by virtue of its objective (intersubjective) validity for the domain of rational beings. The objectivity of the moral law, moreover, would distinguish it from *maxims* that Kant describes as "subjective" principles of action.[73] The difference of categorical and hypothetical prescriptions would thus reflect the differing *modal* status of the (semantical) rules governing one's reasons for acting.[74] Categorical imperatives would be "apodictic" whether they are "formally hypothetical or categorical," writes Beck, since they are directed to one as "a practically rational being regardless of his specific desires."[75] "Assertoric" imperatives of prudence, conversely, oblige one in virtue of subjective desires; and even if such desires were necessary, a priori (assuming one could cognitively specify the imaginative ideal of happiness) they would not generate apodictic imperatives in the Kantian sense of the term. For the "logical necessity" characterizing categorical imperatives designates the synthetic structure of practical (moral) judgment in which the interpretation of one's best reasons is determined a priori by the will (*der Wille*) of a rational being. For Kant, apodictic imperatives show the synthetic, a priori necessity of "the universal lawful form" of my maxims.[76]

THE "OBJECTIVE NECESSITY" OF CATEGORICAL IMPERATIVES

If Kant has succeeded in avoiding one horn of the dilemma, he must yet face the other, for although a modal distinction of categorical imperatives preserves the coherence of dutiful action, it imposes an insuperable burden of proof. For if imperatives are distinguished not by the sense of "ought" (*Sollen*) invoked (which remains constant in all practical prescriptions of the logical form 'O(p)') but, rather, by the modal status of the rules governing the formation of maxims, Kant must show why our maxims "*must* be chosen as if they had to hold as universal laws of nature."[77] Since the concept of an absolutely good will is not defined simply in terms of morality, there is no formal inconsistency in denying that our wills are subject to the categorical imperative. For Kant, the logical correlation of the concept of "absolutely good will" and the concept of a will "whose maxim can always have as its content itself as a universal law" is synthetic, established by a third, pure cognition of the positive conception of freedom, i.e., of autonomy.[78] Autonomy plays a role analogous to that of the pure categories of the understanding in the *Critique of Pure Reason*, although, as an "idea of reason," it does not, strictly speaking, admit of a transcendental deduction.[79]

In his discussion of the third antinomy of the *First Critique*, Kant demonstrated that the idea of "noumenal" freedom is consistent with the supposition of universal empirical determinism. Of the "negative freedom" from sensuous determination (as a logical possibility) there springs, writes Kant, "a *positive* concept, which as positive, is richer and more fruitful," i.e., the concept of pure, autonomous agency.[80] In Kant's words:

> The moral law shows its reality, in a manner which is sufficient even from the point of view of the *critique* of theoretical reason,

in adding a positive characteristic to a causality which so far has been conceived only negatively and the possibility of which, although incomprehensible to theoretical reason, had yet to be assumed by it. This positive characteristic is the conception of reason as immediately determining the will (through the condition that a universal form can be given to its maxims as laws). Thus, for the first time, the moral law can give objective (though only practical) reality to reason which always hitherto had to transcend all possible experience when it put its Ideas to a theoretical use.[81]

Freedom is the *ratio essendi* of the moral law, even as the moral law is regarded as the *ratio cognoscendi* of freedom.[82] In the *Groundwork*, Kant assumes that "morality, together with its principle, follows by a mere analysis of the concept of freedom," and in the *Second Critique*, Kant writes that "freedom and unconditional practical law reciprocally imply each other."[83] Through the autonomy of *Wille*, writes Beck, *Willkür* "supplements its negative freedom with a positive freedom which comes from submission to its own idealized nature as a purely rational will. . . . *Willkür* participates in this autonomy to the degree that its negative freedom vis-a-vis nature is exercised in adherence to the law of pure practical reason."[84]

Yet, as Kant himself recognizes, freedom remains "a mere idea: its objective validity can in no way be exhibited by reference to laws of nature and consequently cannot be exhibited in any possible experience. . . . The idea of freedom can never admit of full comprehension, or indeed of insight, since it can never by any analogy have an example falling under it."[85] The idea of an unschematized *causa noumenon* remains theoretically "incomprehensible," for the pure category of causation is cognitively applicable only to the sensory manifold of experience. The idea of an "intelligible" or "supersensuous" realm as the archetype of the sensuous world subject to the autonomy of pure, practical reason is never, as such, the "object" of experience.[86]

Kant cannot, then, proceed to justify the moral law from an analysis of the conditions of the possibility of our "moral experience." Yet if no action description can be conceived as exemplifying the autonomy of *Wille*, one wonders if the idea of universal law suffices for the objective determination of action. Or, with respect to the subsumption of the individual *casus* of action, must one conclude that freedom as an idea of reason is no more semantically definite than happiness as an ideal of the imagination?

Although the exemplary status of the noumenal realm remains problematic in the *Groundwork*, a somewhat different argument is offered in the *Second Critique*.[87] For while in the former Kant argues as if the principle of the moral law were justified in the appeal to an intelligible realm, in the latter Kant assumes that the principle requires no deduction. The synthetic, a priori principle is presumed, and the idea of freedom is itself "deduced." The moral law (as a constitutive determination of subjective, material maxims) is "given, as an apodictically certain fact, as it were, of pure reason, a fact of which we are a priori conscious."[88]

One must assume, then, that the condition of its givenness, the autonomous "faculty" of will as the *ratio essendi* of the moral law, is likewise given. Kant can thus speak at once of the "fact wherein pure reason shows itself to be practical" as "autonomy in the principle of morality."[89] The consciousness that we have, a priori, of the moral law is "merely the self-consciousness of a pure practical reason, and thus identical with the positive concept of freedom," i.e., with the concept of autonomy.[90]

The self-reflection of a pure practical reason exhibits its idealized nature as *Wille* as the supreme formal condition of constructing maxims: "will as a law unto itself."[91] So construed, the "fact of pure reason" discloses the causality of a mere idea, i.e., of the positive concept of freedom in generating a "moral interest" so as to "determine sensibility in accordance with rational principles."[92] Yet, Kant insists, "the law is not valid for us because it interests us . . . the law interests us because it is valid for us as men in virtue of having sprung from our will as intelligence and so from our proper self."[93]

The *quaestio facti* assumed in Kantian deductions is thus resolved in our reflective apprehension of "a pure practical reason," that is, "autonomy." One's independence of the "heteronomy of efficient causes," as the condition sine qua non of reason "conceiving itself as practical" (and indeed of rational principles generally), implies that "reason must look upon itself as the author of its own principles," i.e., of "laws, which, being independent of nature, are not empirical but have their ground in reason alone."[94] For "freedom of the will" is not "lawless," the idea of "a cause operating without any laws whatsoever" being a *contradictio in adjecto*.[95]

The formal, a priori determination of the will (as "a law unto itself") expresses only "the principle of acting on no maxim other than one which can have for its object itself as at the same time a universal law." This, writes Kant, "is precisely the formula of the categorical imperative and the principle of morality. Thus a free will and a will under moral laws are one and the same."[96] For to "the idea of freedom there is inseparably attached the concept of *autonomy*, and to this in turn the universal principle of morality—a principle which in Idea forms the ground for all actions of rational beings, just as the law of nature does for all appearances."[97]

Yet we must tarry here a moment, for the latter inference is by no means perspicuous. Our apprehension of the "fact of pure reason," of reason legislating autonomously for its practical office, does not permit the immediate inference that one's maxims must emulate the formal universality of empirical (natural) laws. When, in accordance with the reflective explication of the autonomous *Wille*, one "sets aside all matter—that is, all knowledge of objects—there remains nothing over for me except its form."[98] Yet what "remains" is precisely what we have described as (i) the pure form of law (of *Sollen*), which must be distinguished from (ii) the semantical rule specifying my (moral) reasons for acting.

Lest we incur the onus of regressively construing "ought," we cannot simply derive (ii) from (i) as Kant seems to believe. For the occurrence of the pure form of ought (in practical prescriptions of the form 'O(p)') does not, of itself, entail the universality of one's maxims—much less the uniformity of one's actions.[99] Satisfying the formal requirement of practical prescription attests in itself to the "fact of pure reason" (i.e., to reason's practical office), so that Kant cannot merely assume that the "pure form of law" expressed in the formal principle of practical prescription is *necessarily* specified by the principle of morality.

A semantical lacuna in Kant's argument thus looms between the universal necessity of acting in accordance with one's best reasons (implied by the practically rational sense of "ought") and the specification of one's reasons in terms of universalizable maxims. As the "Analytic of Empirical Practical Reason" identifies the formal requirement of "acting in accordance with my greatest good" with "seeking my own happiness" (thus confusing the formal syntax and semantics of practical judgment), so the "Analytic of Pure Practical Reason" illicitly identifies the pure form of law with the "universal lawful form of the maxims of the will."[100]

Once, however, we admit that what I "ought" to do and what it is "dutiful" (morally) for me to do are not logically coextensive, we can no longer regard "a free will and a will under moral laws" as "one and the same." Indeed, the submission of the spontaneous *Willkür* to the universal legislation of *Wille* (i.e., of a pure practical reason) is expressed in the formal delimitation of transcendental freedom by *Sollen*. What Kant says of moral imperatives pertains no less to practical legislation in general:

> No matter how many natural grounds or how many sensuous impulses may impel me to *will*, they can never give rise to the *"ought"* [*Sollen*], but only to a willing which, while very far from being necessary, is always conditioned; and the "ought" pronounced by reason confronts such willing with a limit and an end,—nay more, forbids or authorizes it.[101]

If "we cannot say of anything in nature that it ought to be other than what it actually is in all its temporal relations," *the very possibility* of practical reason exhibits one's freedom from the "heteronomy of efficient causes."[102] Yet this implies that autonomy, regarded as "the property which will has of being a law to itself," would not be *uniquely* specified by the "universal principle of morality."[103] For forming and acting upon my best judgment in accordance with the formal principle 'O(p)' fulfills the stipulation of autonomy that will be a law unto itself, so that, pace Hume, reason cannot be regarded merely as "a slave of the passions." Kant himself admits that

> freedom of the will [*Willkür*] is of a wholly unique nature in that an incentive can determine the will to an action *only so far as the individual has incorporated it into his maxim* (has made it the general rule in accordance with which he will conduct himself); only thus can an incentive, whatever it may be, co-exist with the absolute spontaneity of the will (*i.e.*, freedom).[104]

One must, that is, distinguish the agent who deems the incentive of rational self-love to be her best reason for acting from the *arbitrium brutum* of one so overwhelmed by passion as to be incapable of forming maxims.[105] Moral "evil," indeed, "is possible only as a determination of the free will," for, as Kant remarks in *Religion within the Limits of Reason Alone*,

> the distinction between a good man and one who is evil cannot lie in the difference between the incentives which they adopt into their maxim (not in the content of the maxim), but rather must depend upon *subordination* (the form of the maxim), *i.e.*, *which of the two incentives he makes the condition of the other*. Consequently man (even the best) is evil only in that he reverses the moral order of the incentives when he adopts them into his maxim.[106]

An evil agent may thus honor the maxim of promise keeping *per accidens*, for the sake of an ulterior end, so that his "evil" rests not in his failure to comply with a "universalizable" maxim but, rather, in failing to regard the universality of his maxim as constituting his best reason (incentive) for acting. In this sense, as Beck observes, "even the evil will is autonomous," reflecting one's best judgment.[107]

We may concur with Kant that reflective apprehension of the self-legislative will implies that "to the idea of freedom there is inseparably attached the concept of autonomy."[108] Yet the assumption that a lawless transcendental freedom would be "self-contradictory" (since the "concept of causality carries with it that of laws [*Gesetze*]") fails to justify the further inference that "morality, together with its principle, follows by a mere analysis of the concept of freedom."[109] Since the sense of "ought" is not uniquely determined by the moral law, neither can its occurrence, as the "fact of pure reason," suffice for the justification of *Moralität*. Freedom must consequently be regarded as the *ratio essendi* of the autonomous determination of *Willkür*, and conversely, the *moral* specification of one's best reason(s) as a "*ratio cognoscendi*" of freedom, yet not uniquely so. For *Sollen* may likewise operate upon nonmoral specifications of intentional action (as signified in 'p').

Indeed, the mere occurrence of the practical "ought" satisfies reason's "theoretical interest" in conceiving a totality of conditions in the resolution of the third antinomy. For this "architectonic interest of reason," fulfilled in the supposition of a *causa noumenon* as an unconditioned condition, permits Kant to assert the truth of both the thesis and the antithesis of the antinomy, i.e., that action is (empirically) determined, yet (transcendentally) free.[110] Yet if this is so, freedom cannot serve as an independent "credential for the moral law," for the "principle of the deduction of freedom as a causality of pure reason" cannot simply be assumed as "a sufficient substitute for any a priori justification" of the moral law.[111] If the "positive characteristic" of freedom in the "conception of reason as immediately determining the will" is satisfied by the possibility of *Sollen*, of *Wille* practically legislating in accordance with 'O(p)', one cannot assume that the autonomy of *Wille* necessarily implies that "a universal form be given to its maxims as laws."[112]

We may say, then, that freedom and autonomy are "reciprocal concepts" without thereby assuming that one must "act as if the maxim of your action were to become through your will a universal law of nature."[113] Conceiving "conformity to law in general" in terms of "the production of effects" or empirical events, Kant treats the "formula of the law of nature" as if it were the subjective correlate of the universal, empirical laws of nature (as construed in his transcendental idealism).[114] Yet while universal, natural laws govern the production of empirical *events*, the formal universality of practical law (as expressed in prescriptive judgments of the form 'O(p)') pertains to intentional *action descriptions* (intensionally construed in terms of the "best reason(s)" of the agent in question). "Causality" thus functions analogically in the practical realm, for while it is true that *all* rational agents ought to act in accordance with their best reasons, it does not follow that one's best reason(s) will necessarily be expressed in common moral maxims or uniform behavior.

THE SUFFICIENCY OF MORAL PRESCRIPTION

In the preceding section, I argued that Kant's critique of practical reason, while adumbrating the "positive" conception of freedom (autonomy), fails to justify the objective necessity of the moral law. For the transcendence of the will does not imply the universal dominion of the moral law. For the Romantics, indeed, one "stands above nature as her author and judge," yet, as Beck remarks, "the judge has lost his law." "[W]ith Herder and others," the Kantian synthesis of *Moralität* "anchored . . . in the abstractly personal," is only "an unstable mixture of rationalism and subjectivism. The development was to be completed . . . only by seeing the concretely personal, historical man as the source of law." The "organic" conception of a harmonious "kingdom of ends" is attenuated in the Romantic mythos of the State—of *"Zeitgeist, Volkgeist,* and *Schwärmerei."*[115]

Kant's exaltation of autonomy thus proves to be a dubious blessing. For "if man is autonomous," writes Steven Lukes, "why should not the very choice of values, of the very criteria of evaluation, be up to him?"[116] As we shall see in Part Two, for John Rawls our "rational autonomy" is modeled upon Kantian "hypothetical imperatives" that require merely that our choices be prudent or rationally coherent. Moral maxims are represented as the construction of suitably delimited hypothetical choice, so that, while rational choosers may will "under moral laws," their subjection is "problematic" rather than "apodictic." For J. L. Mackie, indeed, the "universalizability of moral judgments . . . does not impose any rational constraints on choices of action or defensible patterns of behaviour," for one is "logically free to opt out of the moral language game."[117]

Yet our "logical freedom" to opt out of the moral language game does not of itself betoken relativism, for one's "best reason(s)" might still be fulfilled by the moral law. One might yet take up the Kantian banner; for if, as Kant assumes, only moral maxims express "our proper self," only such maxims would suffice as the expression of our rational autonomy.[118] While denying "that morality, together with its principle, follows by *mere analysis* of the concept of freedom," one might nonetheless contend that *if* one acts autonomously, one falls under the moral law.[119]

So one acts "heteronomously," Kant might argue, if "practical reason (the will) . . . administer[s] an alien interest," i.e., sensuous inclination, in place of simply manifesting "its own sovereign authority as the supreme maker of law."[120] Yet even if one were to concur that our "proper, intelligible self" is expressed in the moral law, one could not merely assume that the moral law sufficed for the objective determination of action. For Kant must not only show that one's best reason(s) necessarily abstract from experience; he must likewise show that action may be determined "solely on moral grounds and on the thought of one's duty."[121] If, that is, moral and evil maxims are distinguished by their form rather than their material content, the formal subordination of the incentive of rational self-love to the moral law must *suffice* for the determination of action.

Acting solely "from the motive of duty" fails, however, to discriminate between the "moral" maxim "Always act benevolently," and its contrary (e.g., "Never act benevolently"). For both maxims satisfy the formal, regulative constraint of universality, and may be adopted without formal inconsistency. Inasmuch as I may aspire to villainy yet not incur the onus of inconsistency, the mere *form* of my maxims will not suffice for the relevant discrimination of actions. Finally, one must admit that the *material* specification of our maxims functions constitutively in the rationalization of moral action. As Kant himself concedes, if our Mephistophelean maxim were "a universal law of nature, mankind could get on perfectly well—better no doubt than if everybody prates about sympathy and good will, and even takes pains, on occasion, to practice them, but on the other hand cheats where he can, traffics in human rights, or violates them in other ways."[122]

Yet Kant insists that, "although it is possible that a universal law of nature could subsist in harmony with this maxim, it is impossible to *will* that such a principle should hold everywhere as a law of nature."[123] In the case of "imperfect duties" such as benevolence, the necessity of action arises not from the conceptual but from the volitional contradiction of entertaining its contrary. One's choice is determined by the material and not the formal difference of the maxims "Always act benevolently" and "Never act benevolently."

Even here, however, Kant is not entirely consistent; for in the *Groundwork* the "impossibility" of adopting our Mephistophelean maxim rests in regard for one's "dear self," since "many a situation might arise in which [one] needed love and sympathy from others, and in which, by such a law of nature sprung from his own will, he would rob himself of all hope of the help he wants for himself."[124] Yet having recourse to "personal wisdom" (*Privatklugheit*) in justifying benevolence renders the determination of action contingent upon the semantical indefiniteness of the material, practical principle of rational self-love. Duty would cease to be an objective, practical law precisely as one "makes the incentive of self-love and its inclinations the condition of obedience to the moral law."[125]

Although Kant nods on occasion in invoking rational self-love, characteristically he refers to the "material" interpretation of the categorical imperative, in which one's maxims are determined by "rational nature as an end in itself."[126] Kant assumes that the *formal* stipulation of the universalizability of one's maxims implies *materially* that a "rational being, as by his very nature an end and consequently an end in himself, must serve for every maxim as a condition limiting all merely relative and arbitrary ends." The union of these various "formulations of precisely the same law" is expressed in the "complete determination" of maxims, providing that "all maxims as proceeding from our own making of law ought to harmonize with a possible kingdom of ends as a kingdom of nature."[127]

The correlation of the "formal, material, and complete" determinations of the moral law is regrettably obscure and can hardly be envisioned as "analytical" (if, indeed, the formal determination is constitutively specified in the latter determinations so as to suffice for the objective determination of action). We can but seek to weave the strains of Kant's argument into a coherent whole. For Kant, "autonomy in morals" is reflectively apprehended as a "fact of pure reason." Yet since there is no empirical intuition corresponding to the moral law, the "fact of pure reason" can be nothing other than the expression of the rational autonomy of *Wille*, i.e., of reason legislating a priori for its own practical office. The consciousness that we have a priori of the moral law is "merely the self-consciousness of a pure practical reason . . . identical with the positive concept of freedom [autonomy]."[128]

The self-reflection of a pure practical reason discloses the idealized nature of *Willkür*, i.e., *der Wille*, as the supreme, formal principle of subjective maxims. As the *ratio essendi* of the moral law, *Wille* is not "produced" (*bewirkender*), but rather revealed as a "self-existent" (*selbständiger*) end in the formation of maxims. Certain maxims that may be consistently universalized could thus not consistently be willed if they fail to express the reflective valorization of our "rational nature" as an "end in itself," limiting "all merely relative and arbitrary ends." Benevolence commends itself inasmuch as it expresses our rational nature as "members of an intelligible world" disclosed through the positive concept of freedom as the ground of constructing material maxims.

Since the reflective exhibition of *Wille* represents the self-reflection of a "rational being in general," one prescribes as if from the perspective of a "kingdom of ends," displaying one's membership in a "moral commonwealth." For insofar as one "necessarily conceives [one's] own existence" as an end in itself, the idea of rational nature as an end in itself is "a *subjective* principle of human actions." Yet since "every other rational being conceives his existence on the same rational ground which is valid also for me . . . it is at the same time an *objective* principle."[129] Our rational autonomy would thus imply that "our own making of law ought to harmonize with a possible kingdom of ends."[130]

In Kant's words,

> [T]o say that in using means to every end, I ought to restrict my maxim by the condition that it should also be universally valid as a law for every subject is just the same as to say this—that a subject of ends, namely, a rational being himself, must be made the ground for all maxims of actions, never *merely* as a means, but as a supreme condition restricting the use of every means— that is, always also as an end.[131]

In this fashion, "a world of rational beings (*mundus intelligibilis*) is possible as a kingdom of ends—possible, that is, through the making of their own laws by all persons as its members."[132]

Yet the supposition of "the sublimity of our own nature" is, as we have seen, not a valid consequence of merely "restricting my maxim by the condition that it should also be universally valid as a law for every subject."[133] For even our Mephistophelean maxim fulfilled this formal stipulation. Rejection of our Mephistophelean maxim, indeed, presumes that formally universalizable maxims should be distinguished with respect to the moral incentive of recognizing our "unconditioned and incomparable worth." The maxim "Never act benevolently" could not then be the expression of "our law-making which determines all value" and wherein lies the sublimity of the autonomous *Wille,* which Kant depicts as "the ground of the dignity of human nature and of every rational nature."[134] For "it is not in so far as he is *subject* to the law that he has sublimity, but rather in so far as, in regard to this very same law, he is at the same time its *author* and is subordinated to it only on this ground."[135]

As we have seen in the third section, however, our authorship of practical judgments (exhibiting our autonomy) need not be restricted to the text of the moral law (in its purely formal determination). For if the autonomy of *Wille* is expressed in the possibility of practical prescription, i.e., in accordance with the mere form of law 'O(p),' and if, as Kant assumes, the sublimity of the will derives from its autonomy, the "dignity" of *Wille* would be logically antecedent to its expression in the formal universalization of one's maxims, precedence being ceded thus to the "material," rather than "formal," expression of the categorical imperative.

Kant's invocation of the "dignity of human nature" is, alas, finally a trace rather than an argument—a tantalizing hint of what Godot might say. For Kant fails to show that "reverence for a mere Idea" ("the dignity of humanity") *must* "function as an inflexible precept of the will."[136] Aspiring to a purely formal legitimation of *Moralität*, Kant has severed us from the very stuff of morals. To his heirs, reason would appear increasingly as a "paralysed force, gesture without motion."[137]

NOTES TO CHAPTER 2

1. Kant, *Critique of Practical Reason*, 86.

2. T. S. Eliot, "Journey of the Magi," in *The Complete Poems and Plays* (New York: Harcourt, Brace and World, 1958), 68.

3. Aristotle *Nicomachean Ethics* 1103a10; *Eudemian Ethics* 1220a39–b3; Kant, *Groundwork*, 411 (34). The allusion is to William Butler Yeats, "The Second Coming," in *The Collected Poems of W. B. Yeats* (New York: Macmillan, 1956), 184–85.

4. Thomas Hobbes, *Leviathan*, ed. C. B. Macpherson (Baltimore: Penguin Books, 1968), chap. 11, 160.

5. Cf. Thomas Hobbes, *Human Nature: Or the Fundamental Elements of Policy*, in *British Moralists*, 1: (17), 15; *Leviathan*, chap. 6, 127–28; and *Of Liberty and Necessity*, in *British Moralists*, 1: (96–97), 66–68.

6. Hobbes, *Leviathan*, chap. 8, 139.

7. David Hume, *An Inquiry Concerning the Principles of Morals*, ed. Charles W. Hendel (New York: Macmillan, 1957), 95, n. 6, 102.

8. Hume, *A Treatise of Human Nature*, in *British Moralists*, 2: (507), 20.

9. Ibid., (506), 20.

10. Hume, *An Inquiry Concerning the Principles of Morals*, 51, 93–94.

11. Ibid., 102–103.

12. Ibid., 97, 99.

13. Ibid., 93, 95. For a perceptive interpretation of the triumph of purposive or instrumental rationality in modernity, see Jürgen Habermas's critique of Weberian *Zweckrationalität* in *The Theory of Communicative Action*, trans. Thomas McCarthy (Boston: Beacon Press, 1984), 1:143–271.

14. Immanuel Kant, *Religion within the Limits of Reason Alone*, trans. Theodore M. Greene and Hoyt H. Hudson (New York: Harper and Row, 1960), 31.

15. Kant, *Groundwork*, 416 n. (42 n.)

16. Kant, *Critique of Practical Reason*, 36.

17. Immanuel Kant, *The Metaphysical Elements of Justice*, pt. 1 of *The Metaphysics of Morals*, trans. John Ladd (Indianapolis: Bobbs-Merrill, 1965), 225 (pagination is that of the Prussian Academy edition, vol. 6).

18. Kant, *Groundwork*, 414 (40).

19. Ibid.

20. Ibid., 414 (40), 437 (82).

21. Anscombe, "Thought and Action in Aristotle," 67–69.

22. Kant, *Groundwork*, 414 (40).

23. Ibid., 413 (37), 417 (45) (emphasis added).

24. Ibid., 421 (52).

25. See J. L. Ackrill's analysis in "Aristotle on Action," in *Essays on Aristotle's Ethics*, 100; Sophocles *Antigone*, lines 555–61, p. 138.

26. Kant, *Groundwork*, 415 (40).

27. T. S. Eliot, "Gerontion," in *The Complete Poems and Plays*, 21.

28. Kant, *Critique of Practical Reason*, 22.

29. Lewis White Beck, *A Commentary on Kant's Critique of Practical Reason* (Chicago: University of Chicago Press, 1960), 100.

30. Kant, *Critique of Practical Reason*, 73; *Groundwork*, 413 (38).

31. Kant, *Critique of Practical Reason*, 31–32.

32. See our discussion in chapter 1, section ii.

33. Kant, *Groundwork*, 415 (40).

34. Ibid., 415–16 (42–43).

35. Ibid., 418 (46).

36. Ibid., 417–18 (45–46) (emphasis added).

37. Ibid., 418 (47).

38. Ibid.; cf. *Critique of Practical Reason*, 36.

39. Kant, *Critique of Practical Reason*, 36.

40. Ibid., 45, 47.

41. H. J. Paton, *The Categorical Imperative: A Study in Kant's Moral Philosophy* (Philadelphia: University of Pennsylvania Press, 1948), 126.

42. Beck, *A Commentary on Kant's Critique of Practical Reason*, 86, n. 26.

43. Paton, *The Categorical Imperative*, 126.

44. Ibid.

45. Kant, *Groundwork*, 418 (46).

46. Ibid., 414 (40), 418 (47).

47. Alan Donagan, *The Theory of Morality* (Chicago: University of Chicago Press, 1977), 214–15.

48. Catullus, *The Poems of Catullus*, trans. Peter Whigham (Baltimore, Penguin Books, 1966), (85), 197.

49. Kant, *Groundwork*, 419 (48). See our analysis in chapter 5, 85–88.

50. Ibid., 392 (xiv).

51. Ibid., 415 (41).

52. Ibid., 446 (97).

53. Ibid., 390 (viii).

54. Ibid., 414 (39).

55. Foot, "Morality as a System of Hypothetical Imperatives," 162.

56. Kant, *Groundwork*, 419 (49).

57. See Beck, *A Commentary on Kant's Critique of Practical Reason*, 84–88.
58. Foot, "Morality as a System of Hypothetical Imperatives," 161.
59. Bernard Williams, "Ought and Moral Obligation," in *Moral Luck*, 117.
60. Ibid., 115–17.
61. Ibid., 117.
62. David Ross, *The Right and the Good* (Oxford: Clarendon Press, 1930), 5.
63. Stephan Körner, *Kant* (New Haven: Yale University Press, 1955), 131–32.
64. Kant, *Groundwork*, 413 n. (38 n.); cf. also 447–53 (100–110), 460 n. (122 n).
65. Kant, *Groundwork*, 419 (49).
66. Ibid., 413 n. (38 n.).
67. See Donald Davidson, *Essays on Actions and Events* (Oxford: Clarendon Press, 1980), 9.
68. Kant, *Groundwork*, 406 (25).
69. Ibid., 419 (49) (emphasis added).
70. Ibid., 421 (52).
71. Ibid., 413 (37–38).
72. Ibid., 414 (39).
73. Ibid., 421 n. (51 n.).
74. For the relevance of the modal distinction of hypothetical and categorical imperatives, see Beck, *A Commentary on Kant's Critique of Practical Reason*, 87–88.
75. Ibid., 88.
76. Immanuel Kant, *Critique of Pure Reason*, trans. Norman Kemp Smith (New York: St. Martin's Press, 1929), A76, B101; *Critique of Practical Reason*, 48.
77. Kant, *Groundwork*, 436 (80) (emphasis added).
78. Kant, *Critique of Practical Reason*, 43–50; *Groundwork*, 446–47 (98–99).
79. Kant, *Critique of Practical Reason*, 47.
80. Kant, *Groundwork*, 446–47 (97–98).
81. Kant, *Critique of Practical Reason*, 48 (the translation is by Stephan Körner, in *Kant*, 154).
82. Ibid., 5.
83. Kant, *Groundwork*, 447 (98–99); *Critique of Practical Reason*, 29.
84. Beck, *A Commentary on Kant's Critique of Practical Reason*, 180.
85. Kant, *Groundwork*, 459 (120); *Critique of Practical Reason*, 47.
86. Kant, *Critique of Practical Reason*, 43–44.
87. See Beck's analysis in *A Commentary on Kant's Critique of Practical Reason*, 170–75.
88. Kant, *Critique of Practical Reason*, 47.
89. Ibid., 42.
90. Ibid., 29, 42.
91. Kant, *Groundwork*, 447 (98).
92. Ibid., 460–61 (122–23).
93. Ibid.

94. Ibid., 446 (98), 448 (101), 452 (109), 458 (119).

95. Ibid., 446–47 (98); *Religion within the Limits of Reason Alone*, 30.

96. Kant, *Groundwork*, 447 (98).

97. Ibid., 452–53 (109); *Critique of Practical Reason*, 47.

98. Kant, *Groundwork*, 462 (126).

99. In bk. 1, chap. 1 of the *Critique of Practical Reason* (and in the *Metaphysics of Morals*), Kant acknowledges that the universalizability of maxims is consistent with "variety in the rule" governing specific actions, but in the following chapter, Kant assumes that actions themselves are universalized in accordance with "the form of a natural law" (20, 69–70).

100. Kant, *Critique of Practical Reason*, 48.

101. Kant, *Critique of Pure Reason*, A548, B576.

102. Ibid., A547, B575.

103. Kant, *Groundwork*, 452–53 (109).

104. Kant, *Religion within the Limits of Reason Alone*, 19.

105. Kant, *Critique of Pure Reason*, A534, B562.

106. Kant, *Religion within the Limits of Reason Alone*, 31.

107. Beck, *A Commentary on Kant's Critique of Practical Reason*, 200.

108. Kant, *Groundwork*, 452–53 (109).

109. Ibid., 446–47 (97–99).

110. Kant, *Critique of Pure Reason*, A474, B502–503. See Beck, *A Commentary on Kant's Critique of Practical Reason*, 174, 183–86.

111. Kant, *Critique of Practical Reason*, 47–48.

112. Ibid.

113. Ibid., 29.

114. Kant, *Groundwork*, 421 (52).

115. Beck, *A Commentary on Kant's Critique of Practical Reason*, 125.

116. Steven Lukes, *Individualism* (Oxford: Basil Blackwell, 1973), 101.

117. J. L. Mackie, *Ethics: Inventing Right and Wrong*, 99–100.

118. Kant, *Groundwork*, 461 (123).

119. Ibid., 447 (98) (emphasis added).

120. Ibid., 441 (89).

121. Ibid., 407–408 (26–28).

122. Ibid., 423 (56).

123. Ibid., 424 (57).

124. Ibid., 408 (28), 423 (56–57).

125. Kant, *Religion within the Limits of Reason Alone*, 32.

126. Kant, *Groundwork*, 429–30 (66–70), 436 (80).

127. Ibid., 436–37 (80–81).

128. Kant, *Critique of Practical Reason*, 29, 32, 42, 47.

129. Kant, *Groundwork*, 428–29 (66–67).

130. Ibid., 436 (86).

131. Ibid., 438 (83).

132. Ibid., 438–39 (83–84).

133. Kant, *Critique of Practical Reason*, 87.

134. Kant, *Groundwork*, 435–36 (79).

135. Ibid., 439–40 (86–87).

136. Ibid., 439 (85), 460–61 (123). Even as sympathetic a critic as Alan Donagan concedes that "whatever he may have occasionally implied, Kant did not demonstrate a priori that reason must by its very nature prescribe for free and rational beings what the fundamental principle of morality [i.e., respect for persons as ends in themselves] says it must." *The Theory of Morality,* 237.

137. T. S. Eliot, "The Hollow Men," in *The Complete Poems and Plays,* 56.

PART TWO

The Kantian Heritage

Our world, in Weber's words, is "disenchanted"; the majesty of duty, evanescent.[1] For Kant's modern heirs, morality is spun of the very hypothetical imperatives Kant denounced as "vain illusion and splendid misery."[2] In the moral theories of R. M. Hare and John Rawls, Kantian *Moralität* is metamorphosed into the problematic rules of moral discourse. Hare's "universal prescriptivism" imposes formal (impartial) constraints upon prudential choice, while the "Kantian constructivism" of Rawls's rational (prudential) choosers aspires to the ideal of "pure, procedural justice." No longer does prudence represent "the sublimer sensations . . . as good," in the words of Francis Hutcheson.[3] For, though avowedly a "theory of the moral sentiments," Rawls's treatise on justice assumes that "persons in the original position . . . take no interest in one another's interests," while for Hare "the effect of universalizability is to compel us to find principles" impartially maximizing the satisfaction of preferences; "it does not constrain the preferences themselves."[4]

As I will argue in these pages, however, the problematic formulation of the supreme moral law (as the "universalization" of prudence) fails to elude the Hegelian censure of "empty formalism."[5] For the normative theories of Hare and Rawls differ less with respect to the formal than to the material formulation of the moral law, as varying conceptions of moral *experience* are invoked in the material specification of universal maxims. Just as Kant deferred to the "material" interpretation of the categorical imperative (and the notion of respect for persons it presumes), so, I will argue, Hare and Rawls tacitly limit the relevant preferences of agents by variations upon the Kantian theme of "equal respect."

NOTES TO PART TWO

1. Max Weber, "Science as a Vocation," in *From Max Weber: Essays in Sociology*, ed. H. H. Gerth and C. W. Mills (New York: Oxford University Press, 1946), 155.

2. Immanuel Kant, *Werke*, vol. 4, 161, as quoted in Ernst Cassirer, *Rousseau, Kant, Goethe: Two Essays*, trans. James Gutman, Paul Oskar Kristeller, and John Herman Randall, Jr. (Princeton: Princeton University Press, 1945), 24. Cf. J. L. Mackie's remark that "[l]ogically speaking," it is "a decision if you opt into [the moral language game] even if, historically speaking, you have grown up in it and have never thought of thinking otherwise." *Ethics: Inventing Right and Wrong*, 100.

3. Francis Hutcheson, *An Essay on the Nature and Conduct of the Passions and Affections*, in *British Moralists*, 1:(357), 303.

4. Rawls, *A Theory of Justice*, 147; Hare, *Moral Thinking*, 226.

5. Hegel, *Hegel's Philosophy of Right*, pars. 135, 90.

3

The Universal Prescriptivism
of R. M. Hare

*"The final belief is to believe in a fiction, which you know
to be a fiction, there being nothing else. The exquisite truth
is to know that it is a fiction and that you believe in it
willingly."*[1]

WALLACE STEVENS

For Hare, the general rubrics of hypothetical choice theory permit a
comparison of his own "credible" utilitarianism with other systems
of moral reasoning, most notably the rational contractualism of Rawls.
Such theories, as Alan Donagan observes, presume that practical reason, expressed in the form of "Kantian hypothetical imperatives,"
requires that "every rational creature act on principles on which any
rational creature would choose to act if subject to certain conditions."[2]

The "ideal conditions" governing prudential choice in Hare's
universal prescriptivism derive from an analysis of the logical properties of moral concepts. Sincere moral judgments are characterized by
their "universalizability," i.e., "the logical property of being governed
by a universal quantifier and not containing individual constants."[3]
Impartiality is attained by "purely formal means" as I prescribe universally for "all situations just like the one I am considering," and thus
for all situations irrespective of the role I might myself occupy.[4]

While the formal depiction of moral judgments is reminiscent
of Kant, the *content* of moral prescriptions in Hare's "Kantian variety"
of utilitarianism derives from a commensuration of prudential interests in accordance with the classical principle of utility.[5] Utilitarianism
itself is "compounded of two ingredients," writes Hare, "a formal and
a substantial; and the formal element needs only to be rephrased in

51

order to come extremely close to Kant." There is, indeed, "a very close relation between Bentham's 'Everybody is to count for one, nobody for more than one' . . . and Kant's 'Act only on that maxim through which you can at the same time will that it should become a universal law.'"[6]

The Benthamite inflection of universalizability in the "equal respect" accorded the "equal interests of everybody," permits Hare to derive the content of moral theory from a commensuration of the preferences of those whom our actions affect, and it is "an empirical question what these are."[7] Equal weight is accorded the equal interests of those affected, so that I promote the interests of the parties most if I maximize "the total benefits over the entire population." (For a constant population, this is practically equivalent to the average utility principle; where one's decision affects the size of the population, Hare favors the classical or total utility principle.) Accordingly, I am to act in such fashion that I do for each person affected by my actions what I would wish done for me were I "in precisely his situation," and should my actions affect more than one person, to do what I wish, all things considered, to be done for me were I to occupy their respective situations.[8]

Since it is from a "rational point of view" that I offer my universal prescriptions (in "the 'prudential' sense of rational"), morality for the utilitarian can "only be founded on prudence, which has then to be universalized." The thesis of universalizability, Hare argues, implies that I do for others affected by my decision what I wish done to me, were I to have their preferences rather than those that I now have. Hence, qua "author of the moral decision," I am stripped of all desires and likings in prescribing universally, and only as an affected party do my own desires figure. This mental bracketing does not imply that I cease to have desires, likings, or ideals but only that I am forbidden to consider them qua author of the moral decision.[9]

As the hypothetical subject of the desires of all affected parties considered seriatim, I prescribe universally (and overridingly) if, in according equal weight to equal preferences, I seek to satisfy those preferences of comparatively greater intensity. The intrapersonal comparison of preferences of an individual prudential agent thus serves as an effective analogue for the interpersonal comparison of the preferences of different agents. Prudence is universalized as, qua moral author, I prescribe for the maximal satisfaction of all relevant preferences.[10]

Of themselves materially indefinite, the formal, metaethical attributes of moral judgments acquire normative substance for Hare in the calculus of preference satisfaction. Assuming that preference satisfaction is to be maximized, Hare proceeds to distinguish two levels of normative reflection in accordance with an act utilitarianism that, in view of the universalizability of prescriptions, is "practically equivalent" to a rule utilitarianism whose rules vary in specificity: Level 1, or intuitive thinking, consists in principles of ordinary moral reflection of a "general rule-utilitarian" form in terms of which fantastic situations are of little import. Level 2, or critical thinking, is that of the fictive archangelic preceptor whose omniscient prescriptions would be of a "specific rule-utilitarian" form.[11]

Critical thinking consists in one's choosing "under the constraints imposed by the logical properties of the moral concepts and by the non-moral facts, and by nothing else."[12] It is the province of the ideal observer or ideal prescriber, and as such provides the "criterion of rightness" for specific actions, i.e., the optimal satisfaction of preferences. The "prima facie" rules of intuitive reflection, conversely, are justified by their relative acceptance utility, i.e., the likelihood their observance will lead to the performance of "right" actions (those most conducive to optimal preference satisfaction).

Since intuitive thinking is encompassed within a theory of moral reasoning that does not depend upon "substantial moral intuitions," the specter of intuitive relativism is avoided. The commendable economy of Hare's reasoning, indeed, rests in his assumption that the "steps in the argument from universal prescriptivism to utilitarianism were all based on the logic of the concepts involved."[13] Yet the assumption is belied by the logic of the concepts themselves, for the Benthamite construal of universality fails to be justified by appeal to "purely formal considerations."

THE STIPULATION OF UNIVERSALIZABILITY

While acknowledging Kant's inspiration, Hare does not assume that the mere thought of duty entails the universalizability of one's maxims. His "consistent amoralist" may act prudently, albeit immorally. Hare's universal prescriptivism pertains to the domain of moral agents whose choice is subject to the regulative constraint of universalizability. Hare must thus show that the formal requirement that one "act only on that maxim through which you can at the same time will that it should become a universal law" is materially specified by the Benthamite corollary of "equal concern and respect" that "everybody is to count for one, nobody for more than one."[14]

J. L. Mackie has questioned Hare's Benthamite construal of the Kantian dictum, contending that there are logically distinct stages of universalization in moral judgments, each of which implies that relevantly similar cases be treated similarly:

> [T]he first stage rules out as irrelevant only the numerical differ-
> ence between one individual and another; the second stage rules
> out generic differences which one is tempted to regard as morally
> relevant only because of one's particular mental or physical quali-
> ties or condition, one's social status or resources; the third stage
> rules out differences which answer to particular tastes, prefer-
> ences, values, and ideals.[15]

Regarding only "purely numerical differences" as morally irrelevant in the formation of one's maxims implies that any "sincerely
universalized or universalizable prescription" would be such that its
proponent is "ready to apply [it] to himself and to others and to
go on applying [it] in interpersonal situations when the roles are
reversed."[16] Mackie's initial stage thus fulfills the regulative stipulation
of universalizability. For one's judgments may by governed by a universal quantifier without thereby implying that "generic, qualitative
differences" are "irrelevant in principle."

If qualitative differences are not deemed irrelevant in principle,
one can, nonetheless, assume that my "readiness" to apply a universal
prescription would be a function of the "universalization of prudence," as I imaginatively identify with the circumstances (including
the preferences, values, and ideals) of those affected by my actions.
As assumed in Mackie's second stage, differences would "be fairly
regarded as relevant if they look relevant from whichever side you
consider them."[17] Such reciprocity does not, however, preclude one's
recognition of the moral pertinence of generic differences *tout court*.
In Aristotelian ethics, for instance, differing capacities for *aretē* would
imply that relevant differences be impartially respected: one would
never regard *aretē* as the "mean" of pushpin and poetry. Nor can one
infer from the formal generality of moral reasons that all preferences,
values, or ideals should be treated equally. For Aristotle, indeed, the

discrimination of desire (*orexis*) as "rational" (*boulēsis*) and "irrational" (*thumos* and *epithumia*) forbids our adopting the third stage of universality (which implies that one "acquire a hypothetical concern for the satisfaction of the preferences of oneself in [the] hypothetical situation" of one's actions' recipients, and then be "constrained to turn this merely hypothetical concern into an actual concern" for their fulfillment).[18]

Maxims may thus be formally generalized (fulfilling Mackie's initial stages), yet restricted in scope to the domain of moral agents who share a common "knowledge of the good," as expressed, for instance, in the Aristotelian conception of *sunesis*. For Hare has not succeeded in showing that hypothetical choice, subject to the formal constraint of universalizability, suffices to generate a *unique* set of moral prescriptions. Admitting the moral relevance of the initial stages, Mackie contends that the benevolent commensuration of the third stage of Hare's justification of utilitarianism "is no part of the meaning of moral terms or of the special logic of moral thought."[19]

In earlier writings, Hare himself conceded that we are not "morally constrained . . . under penalty of being said not to be thinking morally" to regard the equally intense ideals of others as equal to our own. The fanatic, whose ideals "override all considerations of people's interests," even the fanatic's own, remained Hare's bête noire. Our philosophical musings aspired to "a humbler aim" than a logically impeccable defense of utilitarianism.[20] Hare's teleological suspension of the fanatic thus attests that, "in framing moral judgments that exclude all proper names and indexical constants"—in Mackie's words—we can "still take account of our own distinctive preferences and values and ideals." For at the second stage of universalizability one has no antecedent assurance that the prescriptions of similarly situated agents will themselves be similar. The golden rule is gilded as Mackie invokes Shaw: "Do not do unto others as you would have that they do unto you. Their tastes may not be the same."[21]

Differing tastes may give rise to differing, even incommensurable "moral" prescriptions, each of which pertains to a subset of the domain of moral agents. I might thus prescribe that one is always to honor one's promises, while my utilitarian confrere prescribes that one is only to honor one's promises if the total benefits are thereby maximized (though, curiously, only the former falls under Hare's rubric of moral fanaticism). As Mackie concludes, there are coherent interpretations of morality that satisfy the first and second stages of universalizability yet reject the third stage as "plainly not characteristic of moral thought in general."[22]

The Kantian dictum that one regard one's maxims as if they were a universal law does not, then, imply as a matter of logical inference the commensuration of "particular tastes, preferences, values and ideals." Nor can one assume, as in Hare's later writings, that moral judgments are "universalizable in only one sense," as "a single logical property" is applied progressively in the generation of moral theory.[23] For Hare has not succeeded in showing that the formal, regulative implications of Mackie's initial stages provide for the *materially* sufficient specification of the latter, i.e., that the "right to equal concern and respect" is redeemed, as Hare assumes, "by giving equal weight to the equal interests of everybody," a precept leading "straight to Bentham's formula and to utilitarianism itself."[24]

BENEVOLENT REDUCTION

Hare's construal of the precept of equal respect presumes a "benevolent reduction," in the words of Bernard Williams, of "all interests, ideals, aspirations and desires" to the representative preferences, differing only in degree, of a common ascriptive subject, be it Hare's "archangel" or a "thoroughly rational egoist."[25] Such a benevolent reduction remains problematic, however, inasmuch as it is by no means evident that the ends of different agents are the kind of thing one can intelligibly compare. For if, as Hare assumes, only "perfectly prudent" preferences figure in the utilitarian calculus, we might assume that the best reasons of differing agents would be represented as such.[26] One would, that is, distinguish the array of what Harry Frankfurt terms "first-order desires" from the desire(s) I desire to have, forming my (second-order) volition or will.[27] Yet while the relative duration or intensity of my first-order desires may be a factor in deciding which is finally to form my will, the exercise of my second-order volition (assuming, ex hypothesi, my continence) presumes my judging what I have best reason to do. (As Aristotle recognized, one's best reason[s] may be constituted deliberatively; yet, once constituted, they mark the term of deliberation. Once I assume the moral virtues specify blessedness, I can no longer deliberate about whether I ought to be virtuous.)

Critical thinking thus resolves the "comparison problem" by regarding the second-order volitions of differing agents (expressed *assertorically* in the determination of their best reasons) as if they were the first-order desires of a single agent whose best reasons are still to be determined.[28] What I, as a prudentially rational agent, have best reason(s) to do is represented *problematically* as what a moral author "might" have best reason to do, provided the sums work out. The self is rendered a moral cipher of maximizing utilities, a benevolent reduction representing, in the words of Rawls, "the dissolution of the person as leading to a life expressive of character and of devotion to specific final ends and adopted (or affirmed) values which define the distinctive points of view associated with different (and incommensurable) conceptions of the good."[29]

THE INDETERMINACY OF CRITICAL PRESCRIPTION

Hare's implicit distinction of the orders of intention (relative to the intuitive subject) and justification (relative to the fictive archangel) introduces a further complexity, inasmuch as the "moral feeling" of benevolence may be predicated of either. For, whether benevolence is regarded as "an independent criterion" or as a "mere rephrasing of universalizability," "some degree of benevolence is required" if our "universal prescriber" is to be "positively and equally benevolent to everybody."[30] Yet since the "moral author" is at once an intuitive "moral subject," the moral feeling of benevolence recurs in the description of the latter. Interpreting universalizability in terms of utilitarian benevolence implies that the "benevolent" preference of the moral subject be impartially subsumed in the normative calculus of preference satisfaction as, in William's words, one dispensable "satisfaction among others."[31]

A certain indeterminacy is thereby introduced into the definition of the optimal outcome, for my benevolent preference qua moral author attains material specificity in the commensuration of the preferences of moral subjects, among which figures the moral feeling of benevolence (conceived as a merely possible purpose). Just as the "Kantian Requirement" defined duty regressively, so in Hare's "Kantian variety" of utilitarianism the optimal outcome satisfying 'p' presupposes my preference "that 'p'," even if the latter is but one of my preferences subject to commensuration. As in Leibnitzian monadology, the moral author's feeling of benevolence "mirrors" the selfsame feeling in the moral subject, thereby rendering the outcome necessarily indeterminate.[32]

THE LIMITS OF INTUITIVE PRESCRIPTION

Even were we to concede that a benevolent interpretation of universality is not vacuous, it is still doubtful that the intuitive moral subject would number among Hare's utilitarian cherubim. For it is hardly fanciful to assume that in some circumstances preference satisfaction would be optimally served if prima facie, intuitive moral principles departed from the critical, archangelic precepts. As Sidgwick observed: "The doctrine that Universal Happiness is the ultimate *standard* must not be understood to imply that Universal Benevolence is . . . always the best *motive* of action. For . . . it is not necessarily that the end which gives the criterion of rightness should always be the end at which we consciously aim."[33]

In Hare's Kantian analysis, we might say that the "ultimate standard," i.e., regulative conformity to universal law, need not function "constitutively" in determining one's "motive" or best reason. As Sidgwick reminds us, "If experience shows that the general happiness will be more satisfactorily attained if men frequently act from other motives than pure universal philanthropy, it is obvious that these other motives are to be preferred on Utilitarian principles."[34] My reasons as a moral subject may, then, differ from my reasons as a moral author, for critical reflection, which favors the inculcation of intuitions incorporating "departures from impartiality, is itself impartial," i.e., their "inculcation will be for the best for all concerned impartially."[35] A general respect for rights and considerations of justice, often regarded as antithetical to act utilitarianism, is thus critically vindicated for Hare. Indeed, the prima facie moral principles "of substantial, including procedural, justice in the administration of the law" are likely to be of "the sort dear to deontologists." For the "grounds of selection will be utilitarian; but the principles selected may not themselves look utilitarian at all."[36]

Yet even if benevolence were one's "best motive," it would be so as a consequence of benevolent commensuration, for, as we have seen, the reasons critically justifying one's action (those of our archangelic prescriber) only obliquely rationalize it. The preferences expressed in intuitive prescriptions are not "definitive of the right act," i.e., the optimific outcome, but, rather, are optimally conducive to its occurrence. Differing action descriptions will thus be generated according to the level of prescription. *Critically* 'A' will be described as fulfilling the regulative requirement of universalizability (interpreted in terms of "universal benevolence"), e.g., my promise keeping as a means to the optimal outcome. *Intuitively*, however, 'A' will be described in terms of the intentions most likely to lead to the occurrence of the action critically prescribed, e.g., my promise keeping regarded "deontologically" as an end in itself. Fulfilling the regulative, Benthamite requirement of universality need not constitute a *motive* for acting, especially in cases where the optimal satisfaction of preferences forbids my prescribing critically, i.e., where impartiality is best served by adopting principles that may not themselves "look utilitarian at all."

Critical prescriptions operate upon intuitive prescriptions, so that, in terms of the "metalanguage" of critical prescription, my judgment "I ought to perform 'A' under the description 'd_1'" is true if and only if my performance of 'A', so described, is conducive to the optimal outcome. Intuitive, prima facie principles are never truly "overriding" in themselves, since there is always a further "criterion" or "standard," in Sidgwick's words, to which they must conform, i.e., their acceptance value with respect to the optimal outcome. Omniscient archangels might prescribe that I "ought" (critically) to regard "poetical fictions," such as "One ought (intuitively) always to honor one's promises," *as* "true" or overriding, adding with a wink, "because my beneficent illusion promotes the greater good."

The logical distinction of critical and intuitive senses of "ought" introduces a surprising degree of regimentation of ordinary (intuitive) language for a philosophy aspiring to be based "on linguistic *intuitions* only." Yet the aspiration, alas, is belied by the logic of the concepts themselves. For Hare's "Kantian variety" of utilitarianism, as we have seen, is finally not a mere "restatement of the requirement that moral principles be universalizable." His Benthamite construal of "equal respect" derives not from the formal properties of moral concepts but from a "special and radical" interpretation of benevolence yet to be redeemed.[37]

NOTES TO CHAPTER 3

1. Wallace Stevens, "Adagia," in *Opus Posthumous*, ed. Samuel French Morse (New York: Alfred A. Knopf, 1957), 163.

2. Alan Donagan, *The Theory of Morality*, 215.

3. Hare, *Moral Thinking*, 41.

4. R. M. Hare, "Ethical Theory and Utilitarianism," in *Utilitarianism and Beyond*, ed. Amartya Sen and Bernard Williams (Cambridge: Cambridge University Press, 1982), 25. For Hare, the differentiation of moral judgments presumes not only their "regulative" universalizability but their "overriding" force. Cf. Hare, *Moral Thinking*, 24, 50–61.

5. Hare, "Ethical Theory and Utilitarianism," 37.

6. Hare, *Moral Thinking*, 4.

7. Ibid., 5; and "Rights, Utility, and Universalization: Reply to J. L. Mackie," in *Utility and Rights*, ed. R. G. Frey (Minneapolis: University of Minnesota Press, 1984), 106–20.

8. Hare, "Ethical Theory and Utilitarianism," 26.

9. Ibid., 28–29.

10. Hare, *Moral Thinking*, 110.

11. Hare, "Ethical Theory and Utilitarianism," 31–33.

12. Hare, *Moral Thinking*, 40, 44.

13. Ibid., 40, 176.

14. As Hare himself admits, the objective validity of prudential prescriptions implies that there is a sense "in which [even nonmoral] prudential judgments are universalizable." For "I cannot say 'I ought in my own interest, but you ought not, in your own interest, although we and our situations were precisely similar,'" for, were our situations precisely similar, "your interest and the means to satisfying it would also be the same." Since the criterion of "precise similarity" is satisfied by the assumption that agents act in accordance with their best interests (only thus "ought" they to act), the property of universality, if it is not to figure redundantly in "universal prescriptivism," must be conceived as qualifying the interpretation of my maxims. R. M. Hare, "Do Agents Have to Be Moralists?" in *Gewirth's Ethical Rationalism*, ed. Edward Regis, Jr. (Chicago: University of Chicago Press, 1984), 55.

15. Mackie, *Ethics: Inventing Right and Wrong*, 97.

16. Ibid., 85, 89.

17. Ibid., 90–91.

18. Hare, *Moral Thinking*, 223.

19. Mackie, *Ethics: Inventing Right and Wrong*, 96.

20. R. M. Hare, *Freedom and Reason* (Oxford: Oxford University Press, 1963), 177, 184–85.

21. Mackie, *Ethics: Inventing Right and Wrong*, 89.

22. Ibid., 97.

23. Hare, *Moral Thinking*, 108.

24. Hare, "Rights, Utility, and Universalization: Reply to J. L. Mackie," 106–107. On the supposition of Bentham's reduction, it would be "inevitable," writes Hare, that honoring the precept would lead us to weigh the interests

of different individuals just as a "single thoroughly rational egoist would weigh together his own desires or satisfactions."

25. Bernard Williams, *Ethics and the Limits of Philosophy*, 86.

26. Hare, "Ethical Theory and Utilitarianism," 28.

27. Harry Frankfurt, "Freedom of the Will and the Concept of a Person," *Journal of Philosophy* 68, no.1 (1971): 8.

28. Hare, *Moral Thinking*, 128.

29. Rawls, *A Theory of Justice*, 187; "Social Unity and Primary Goods," in *Utilitarianism and Beyond*, 181. See also Bernard Williams, "A Critique of Utilitarianism" in *Utilitarianism: For and Against*, ed. J. J. C. Smart and Bernard Williams (Cambridge: Cambridge University Press, 1973), 116–17.

30. R. M. Hare, "Rawls' Theory of Justice," in *Reading Rawls*, ed. Norman Daniels (New York: Basic Books, 1975), 93.

31. Williams, "A Critique of Utilitarianism," 116.

32. Cf. A. I. Melden, *Rights in Moral Lives* (Berkeley: University of California Press, 1988), 100.

33. Henry Sidgwick, *The Methods of Ethics*, 7th ed. (Indianapolis: Hackett, 1981), 413 (emphasis added).

34. Ibid.

35. Hare, *Moral Thinking*, 129; "Ethical Theory and Utilitarianism," 34.

36. Hare, *Moral Thinking*, 162.

37. Ibid., 154.

4

The Kantian Constructivism
of John Rawls

"The impossible possible philosophers' man,
The man who has had the time to think enough,
The central man, the human globe, responsive
As a mirror with a voice, the man of glass,
Who in a million diamonds sums us up."[1]

WALLACE STEVENS

Rawls's magisterial interpretation of justice is, in Hare's words, "formally analogous" to his own universal prescriptivism. Yet while Hare seeks to derive the pertinent constraints upon rational (prudent) choice from a metaethical, linguistic analysis, Rawls offers a "more dramatic" and "elaborate" account of their derivation. For his "Kantian constructivism" rests not merely upon the "truths of logic and definition" but upon a conception of moral agents as free and equal rational beings who desire to abide by effective principles of justice "in a well-ordered society."[2]

Rawls's construction of the first principles of justice presumes the interrelation of the "model conceptions" of the moral person and the well-ordered society through the heuristic device of the "original position."[3] As a "third and mediating model conception," the original position represents the "Rational" and "Reasonable" constraints imposed upon prudential choice. The former reflect the "rational autonomy" of the contracting parties, who as agents of construction "are not required to apply, or to be guided by, any prior and antecedent principles of right and justice" in their deliberation.[4] Since no a priori moral law is to be instantiated in the selection of principles, their construction aspires to "pure procedural justice at the highest level" where the outcome of the original position defines "the appropriate principles of justice." The parties are permitted to agree to any possible conception of justice inspired by their prudential assessment of the alternative most likely to promote their respective interests.[5] In this regard, writes Rawls, the conception of rational autonomy "roughly parallels Kant's notion of hypothetical imperatives" (while, as we shall see, "Reasonable" constraints are interpreted in terms of the categorical imperative).[6]

The exercise of deliberative rationality characterized by "sensible principles of rational choice" is not, however, directed to the array of agents' actual interests but is restricted, rather, to those interests uniquely determining agents as free and equal moral persons.[7] As envisaged by Rawls, moral persons exhibit an immanent stratification of volition in terms of which the motivational assumptions of the original position are fixed. Moral persons are thus characterized by two "moral powers" and by two correlative "highest-order interests in realizing and exercising these powers." The initial power is our capacity to form an "effective sense of justice," i.e., the capacity to "understand, to apply and to act from (and not merely in accordance with) the principles of justice." The second moral power is our capacity to "form, to revise, and rationally to pursue a conception of the good." Our "highest-order" interests are regarded as "supremely regulative as well as effective," governing our higher-order interest in sustaining and promoting the realization of our particular conceptions of the good.[8]

Our highest-order interests are specified by our preference for "primary goods," inasmuch as the exercise of rational autonomy in the original position presumes that agents enjoy certain "general all-purpose means" necessary for developing and exercising their two moral powers and for their effective pursuit of a conception of the good over a complete life. As depicted in Rawls's "thin theory of the good," these primary social goods, which "all members of society are presumed to want more of," constitute the minimal motivational content of effective deliberation in the original position.[9]

The lexical ordering of primary social goods presumes that the exercise of "rational autonomy" is subject to the formal constraints of "full autonomy" in a well-ordered society. These constitute the "Reasonable" requirements flowing from our nature as free and equal moral persons: the constraints of the formal concept of right, the veil of ignorance, the symmetry of the parties with respect to one another, and the stipulation that society's "basic structure" is the first subject of justice.[10]

If the parties' "rational autonomy" represents a more restrictive conception of *prudential* choice than that of Hare's universal prescriptivism, the "moral ideal" of "full autonomy" is comparatively richer.[11] For while the formal conception of right implies that the principles of justice are "general in form and universal in application" and are recognized as a "final court of appeal" for the conflicting claims of moral persons, the criterion of "full publicity" is specifically limited to the construction of the principles of justice. Publicly shared beliefs regarding human nature and social institutions afford a "complete justification" of generally acknowledged principles. The constraint of full publicity is not entailed by the mere analysis of moral concepts, argues Rawls, but is rather a "reasonable" supposition for a theory of justice whose first subject is the basic structure of society.[12]

Similarly, the veil of ignorance is invoked to ensure not only the impartiality associated with universalizability (as specified by Mackie's second stage), but unanimity in the selection of principles. Depriving the contracting parties of knowledge of their respective social roles, their acquired and natural advantages, the particular circumstances of their society, and even their values, aims, and particular conceptions of the good, the veil of ignorance permits morally arbitrary contingencies to be "bracketed" for the purposes of deliberation. Since deliberation in the original position is thus restricted to nondiscriminating primary social goods, the parties are symmetrically situated, so that the "deliberation of any one person" becomes "typical of all."[13]

What *is* known under the veil of ignorance, other than general, nondiscriminating facts about society and the preference of agents for primary social goods, is that society is subject to the "circumstances of justice" described by Hume, i.e., the "objective" condition of moderate scarcity, which renders our social cooperation "both possible and necessary," and the "subjective" condition of "mutual disinterest," which assumes that the parties contracting for "mutual advantage" are not bound "by any prior moral ties to each other."[14] Divested of any dominant, predelineated ends or "natural" finality, persons in the original position are presumed to "take no interest in one another's interests." Indeed, for the purposes of deriving the principles of justice, Rawls assumes a "deep opposition of interests," reflecting "maximin" expectations in competitive and uncertain circumstances.[15] In this sense, concludes Rawls, "there is nothing a priori about moral philosophy."[16]

The supposition of mutually disinterested rationality thus accords with the Kantian critique of eudaimonism (the "technical reduction" of prudence).[17] For Rawls assumes not only limited altruism but a multiplicity of morally permissible ends, each "compatible with the full autonomy and rationality of human persons."[18] In *Political Liberalism* he writes that "for political purposes, a plurality of reasonable yet incompatible comprehensive doctrines is the normal result of the exercise of human reason within the framework of the free institutions of a constitutional democratic regime."[19]

The initial situation is thus suitably defined in terms of the formal constraints of the "Rational" and the "Reasonable," so that the construction of the principles of justice fulfills the conditions of pure procedural justice. Just as for Hare prudential prescriptions are delimited by the formal requirements of universalizability, so for Rawls "the Reasonable frames the Rational" in the original position, reflecting the "strict priority" of the "Reasonable" with respect to the "Rational." Yet while for Hare universalizability pertains to the commensuration of agents' desires, likings, and ideals (as expressed in Rawls's "full theory" of the good), the restricted scope of choice in the original position permits Rawls to assert the priority of "the right over the good" as "characteristic of Kantian constructivism."[20] Unanimity is attained not by conflating "all desires into one system of desire" but by attaining an "overlapping consensus of reasonable comprehensive doctrines" that respects the distinction of persons and their multiple and incommensurable conceptions of the good.[21]

Bounded by the aforementioned constraints of the "Reasonable," rationally autonomous agents select the principles of justice that in a well-ordered society allow them to express their "full autonomy."[22] Subject to these formal constraints, hypothetical choice in the original position establishes the consensual primacy of liberty in the lexically ordered principles of justice:

> *First Principle.* Each person is to have an equal right to the most extensive total system of equal basic liberties compatible with a similar system of liberty for all.
> *Second Principle.* Social and economic inequalities are to be arranged so that they are both: (a) to the greatest benefit of the least advantaged, consistent with the just savings principle, and (b) attached to offices and positions open to all under conditions of fair equality of opportunity.[23]

Although Rawls prides himself on his Kantian legacy, dismissing perfectionist doctrines of the good, the derivation of the principles of justice is envisaged within the "scope of an empirical theory." Kant's doctrine of autonomy, writes Rawls, must be "detached from its background in transcendental idealism" and expressed in terms of the "canons of a reasonable empiricism."[24] Kantian constructivism does not, then, interpret the moral law (variously formulated by Kant) as a synthetic, a priori practical judgment.

While in the *Critique of Practical Reason* the moral law is "schematized" through the assumption that one legislates for a "kingdom of ends" (where the Idea or archetype of such a realm "determines our will to impart to the sensuous world the form of a system of rational beings"), the formal requirement of universality is viewed by Rawls as "too slender a basis" for a substantive moral theory.[25] Following Sidgwick's criticism of Kantian formalism, Rawls assumes that the noumenal self can "choose any consistent set of principles" since Kant failed to show that "acting from the moral law expresses our nature in identifiable ways that acting from contrary principles does not."[26]

The "moral ideal" of full autonomy (exhibiting the regulative constraint of universality) must thus be specified through the appropriate "Reasonable" constraints. In Rawls's words, the original position may be construed as a "procedural interpretation of Kant's conception of autonomy and the categorical imperative." No longer the issue of aprioristic legislation, *Moralität* is domesticated, as the principles prescribed for a "kingdom of ends" are *constructed* through the exercise of prudential choice.[27]

Principles deriving their content from general empirical assumptions that phenomenally delimit rational (prudential) choice, i.e., the circumstances of justice and the thin theory of the good, are regarded by Kant as hypothetical imperatives. Yet the modal status of the principles of justice is somewhat obscure in Rawls's analysis. For although conceding that the exercise of rational autonomy generates hypothetical imperatives, Rawls conceives the principles themselves as "categorical imperatives in Kant's sense." To act from the lexically ordered principles of justice is to "act from categorical imperatives," since hypothetical imperatives depend upon "one's having an aim which one need not have as a condition of being a rational human individual."[28]

Since the primary social goods are regarded as general all-purpose means that it is "rational to want whatever else one wants," Rawls argues that the principles of justice do not depend upon merely contingent premises in their derivation.[29] For Kant, however, this is a sufficient difference only of assertoric and problematic *hypothetical* imperatives, where the former are determined by "a purpose which we can presuppose a priori and with certainty to be present in every[one] because it belongs to his very being."[30] Inasmuch as Rawls concurs with Kant that the conception of happiness is necessarily indefinite (thereby precluding a perfectionist doctrine of the good), the principles of justice would "in Kant's sense" be problematic rather than assertoric in modality.

The justification of the principles thus depends upon whether we are entitled to adopt the "Reasonable" constraints that define the original position, for were other procedural constraints shown to be equally reasonable, one would have no assurance, given the problematic structure of reasoning, that rational choosers would select just these principles in resolving problems arising from interpersonal comparisons. Yet Rawls concedes that the justification of the constraints upon hypothetical choice in the original position is neither formally nor materially self-evident. A conception of justice cannot "be deduced from self-evident premises or conditions on principles"; rather, its justification depends upon the "mutual support of many considerations . . . fitting together into one coherent view." Considerations relevant to our arriving at the favored interpretation of the initial situation are introduced through what Rawls terms a method of "reflective equilibrium," in which a moral theory is progressively constructed in the "mutual adjustment of principles and considered judgments." It represents an attempt to encompass within a single scheme both "reasonable philosophical conditions" upon principles and "our considered judgments of justice." Lest the entire issue of reflection be question-begging, the description of the initial situation must represent "generally shared and preferably weak conditions," each of which should by itself be "natural and plausible," if not indeed "innocuous or even trivial."[31]

THE TACIT ROLE OF PREJUDICE[32]

One wonders, however, if the constraints defining the initial situation are as innocuous or trivial as Rawls assumes. In his interpretation of Hume's "circumstances of justice" in part 1 of *A Theory of Justice*, Rawls asserts that the principles of justice cannot be "contingent upon certain social or other conditions," as if one conception "might hold at one stage of culture, a different conception at another." The principles obtain "unconditionally, whatever the circumstances," according to the Kantian interpretation of justice as fairness. In his discussion of the veil of ignorance, Rawls assumes further that the contracting parties do not "know the particular circumstances of their own society," being ignorant of its economic and political status and even of "the level of civilization and culture" it has attained. Provided that the relevant resources are not so plentiful that "schemes of cooperation" are rendered superfluous, nor so limited that our ventures are inevitably doomed, the principles of justice as fairness are not "contingent upon existing desires" or prevalent social conditions.[33] Our conception of the just basic structure of society is thereby accorded legitimacy as a "standard for appraising institutions."[34]

Yet in part 3 Rawls concedes that the principles of justice obtain only if a "certain level of wealth has been attained." For if one might find oneself in a condition of grave poverty once the veil is lifted, the probability of which is unknown under maximin conditions of uncertainty, providing for subsistence might be eminently reasonable. As Rawls acknowledges, until the basic wants of individuals can be satisfied, the relative priority of their interest in liberty cannot be "firmly decided in advance." In accepting the lexical priority of the principles of justice, we are thus not compelled to deny that "the value of liberty depends upon circumstances." The primacy of liberty is, rather, to be conceived as the "long-run tendency of the general conception of justice consistently pursued" under favorable circumstances.[35]

In his later essay "Kantian Constructivism in Moral Theory," these conditions are further specified as pertaining to the "public culture of a democratic society," characterized by a common history and the "tradition embedded in our public life." Our concern is no longer with the moral person *per se* but rather with a conception of the person implicitly affirmed in such a culture. Nor are the principles of justice unconditionally binding "whatever the circumstances," for, concedes Rawls, our aim is finally not to construct a conception of justice suitable for all societies irrespective of their particular historical circumstances. The contractors seek rather to "articulate and to make explicit those shared notions and principles thought to be already latent in common sense."[36]

Since the lexical ordering of primary goods is relative to the prevalence of favorable circumstances in a democratic society "under modern conditions," honoring the formal constraint of finality entails a considerable modification of Hume's circumstances of justice. For under the maximin conditions assumed by Rawls, and if one is limited to a single set of principles obtaining "whatever the circumstances" or stage of culture, it is not unreasonable to suppose that the parties in the original position might prefer welfare to liberty. Even if we concede that the principles of justice obtain only as a long-run tendency, and hence only at a certain stage of development, there seems no reason to believe that liberty is the inevitable *telos*. For might not liberty admit of thresholds of satisfaction just as welfare, such that, once a sufficient degree of the primary good is enjoyed, other goods assume a relative priority? Or if our invoking Hume's circumstances of justice implies that the virtues of "benevolence, or fraternity, or of enlarged affection" are, in the words of Michael Sandel, of "at least correlative status," must we accept that an increment of liberty is always to be preferred to a like increment of benevolence or fraternity?[37]

One cannot assume, then, that the "subjective circumstance" of "limited generosity" necessarily implies a "deep opposition of interests," nor may the supposition of "mutually disinterested rationality" be regarded as a "weak" assumption. As we have seen in our criticism of Kant, the formal, analytic structure of prudential, hypothetical imperatives requires that agents act in accordance with their best reasons (or interests) yet does not of itself imply an egoistic conception of what these interests might be. Rawls's denial of "extensive ties of natural sentiment" is already an interpretation of the agent's good, so that it is a "weak" assumption only relative to a full theory of the good, i.e., one characterized precisely by the denial of Hume's assertion that our "first state" is "justly esteemed [as] social."[38] Yet such a gambit is denied Rawls under the veil of ignorance. For were the veil as thick as Rawls imagines, we would want any compelling reason for believing our ends to be deeply opposed, rather than bound by ties of natural sentiment.

Even the "thin" theory of primary social goods finally depends upon a "thicker" conception of agents' goods, for, as Rawls admits, such putative "non-discriminating" goods cannot be conceived as general means "essential for achieving whatever final ends a comprehensive empirical or historical survey" might show agents "usually or normatively to have in common under all social conditions."[39] Thomas Nagel observes that

> the primary goods are not equally valuable in pursuit of all conceptions of the good. They will serve to advance many differ-

ent individual life plans (some more efficiently than others), but they are less useful in implementing a view that holds a good life to be readily achievable only in a society that works concertedly for the realization of certain higher human capacities and the suppression of baser ones.[40]

The justificatory role played by the thin theory of the good thus depends upon our interpretation of the full theory, at least insofar as a general conception of the good (as a *bonum singulare* rather than *bonum commune*) is assumed in the indexation of primary goods. Yet this is to concede that the premises of the principles of justice are, after all, contingent upon existing desires and prevailing social conditions, since the thin theory lacks the requisite independence of the full theory to justify an unequivocal precedence of right. As Nagel concludes, neither mutual disinterest nor the thin theory of the good are normatively innocent suppositions. "Rawls' minimal conception of the good does not amount to a weak assumption: it depends on a strong assumption of the sufficiency of that reduced conception for the purposes of justice."[41]

A less restrictive, or "thinner," veil of ignorance might, then, suffice for impartiality, permitting agents knowledge of their final ends and conceptions of the good, while denying them knowledge of which individual they might be. Rawls admits that Hume's "judicious spectator" attains a form of impartiality; for, writes Hare of such an "economical veil," if one were ignorant of whether one "is 'a' or 'b'," however selfish one might be, one would lack a motive for favoring principles promoting the interests of 'a' over those of 'b' in cases of conflict.[42] Yet Rawls demurs that depriving an agent of knowledge of her final end is tantamount to depriving her of *any* motive for discriminating among final ends at all. The argument concludes with "a purely formal expression for an expectation that is without meaning."[43] One wonders, though, if much the same criticism does not apply to the ordering of primary goods once their relative significance to the fulfillment of agents' final ends is suppressed.

In aiming at the "thickest possible veil of ignorance," our fictitious contractors are granted only that knowledge representative of their status as free and equal moral persons. For finally the choice of primary social goods rests not upon empirical psychological inquiry but upon a specific "moral" conception of the person, "embodying a certain ideal." The first principles of justice reflect the desire of "rationally autonomous agents" to secure the conditions of the "development and exercise of their moral powers, and their determinate (but unknown) final ends."[44] The formal constraints of the "Reasonable" and the "Rational" thus find their justification not in their innate plausibility—for they are hardly innocuous or trivial assumptions—but rather in their "lucid representation of the notion of freedom" characterizing a "Kantian view."[45]

THE PREJUDICE OF EQUAL RESPECT

In view of the "representative" function of the formal constraints and the doctrine of autonomy inspiring them, it comes as little surprise that the contracting parties would recognize the primacy of liberty. Yet it is not immediately apparent that the *representation* of freedom (such as Kant envisioned in the "Typic of Pure Practical Judgment") can be reconciled with a *constructivist* interpretation depicting the primacy of liberty as the (a posteriori) object of hypothetical choice. For Rawls assumes (i) that in their deliberations, our rational contractors are not compelled to "apply or to be guided by, any . . . antecedent principles of right and justice" and (ii) that they are "moved solely by the highest-order interests in their moral powers" and by their desire to promote their "determinate" yet "unknown final ends."[46] Limited by the constraints of the "Reasonable," rationally autonomous agents construct the principles of justice—a construction that is formally problematic, and logically antecedent to material principles of right and justice.

The parties' "sense of justice," as specified by the formal, "Reasonable" stipulations of full autonomy, thus functions as a purely regulative constraint upon rational (prudential) choice. Yet this is hardly perspicuous. For if among the political goods recognized in a well-ordered society is the realization and development of both moral powers, one wonders why only the latter should be regarded as constitutive of the parties' determinate conception of the good. If, indeed, we assume that Rawls's depiction of fully autonomous citizens is "reasonable," would not the very reasons that *justify* the ideal of the moral person suffice, pari passu, to *explain* the motives of the contracting parties?

Since the original contractors as "moral persons" are characterized by their "moral power" to form an "effective sense of justice," i.e., their capacity to "understand, to apply and *to act from* (and not merely in accordance with) the principles of justice," one can no longer conceive fairness as a purely formal, regulative constraint to which the parties adventitiously adhere. For their "executive and regulative highest-order desire" in the realization of their "moral powers" governs their "higher-order" interests in sustaining and promoting the realization of their *particular* conception of the good. Only "higher-order interests" consistent with their "highest-order interests" can fittingly be described as "reasons" for acting.[47]

The parties' *"higher*-order" interests must accordingly be conformed to their *"highest*-order" interest in fairness (itself specified by their *"highest*-order" interest in the realization of their second moral power, i.e., their capacity to "form, to revise, and rationally to pursue a conception of the good"). For their formal interest in the fair (impartial) comparison of interests presupposes the equal regard of agents' "highest-order" interest in the realization of their moral personality: in *"view of their . . . conception of the person as free and equal,"* agents thus regard themselves as "all equally worthy of being represented," i.e., as moral persons whose "rights in the procedure for choosing principles" must be respected.[48]

Assuming that their "highest-order" interests are "supremely regulative as well as effective," agents' choices in the original position thus exhibit their status *as* "moral persons." In this respect, as Rawls admits, the original position is not "meant to be morally neutral"; rather, it is intended to be fair between "individuals conceived as moral persons with a *right* to equal respect and consideration in the design of their common institutions."[49] The "principles of justice manifest in the basic structure of society [their] desire to treat one another not as means only but as ends in themselves." Only thus do the "lexical priorities of justice represent the value of persons that Kant says is beyond all price."[50]

Yet if one concedes with Rawls that the equal respect owed persons regardless of their social roles is *"fundamental"* (and thus antecedent to the "construction" of rights), one cannot consistently describe the contracting parties as "not required to apply, or to be guided by, any . . . antecedent principles of right and justice."[51] For in applying a "procedural" conception of Kant's "formal" formulation of the "categorical imperative," agents implicitly invoke Kant's "material" formulation. In satisfying the constraints of impartiality, agents must respect one another as "ends in themselves and not merely as means." Indeed, in exhibiting the status of agents as "free and equal moral persons," rationally autonomous choice in the original position displays the "mutual interestedness" of agents in constituting a "kingdom of ends" (in Kant's terms, the "complete determination of the categorical imperative").[52]

As the expression of "rational autonomy," prudential choice is thus intrinsically limited by respect for the equal worth of rational agents, recalling the Aristotelian distinction of *technē* (instrumental reasoning) and *phronēsis* (the expression of moral "self-knowledge" in *praxis*). The ideally regulative status of the moral personality is reflectively exhibited, rather than "constructed," in hypothetical choice. Yet while the theory of justice provides a rendering of these ideas, Rawls's empiricist interpretation of Kant implies that we "cannot start out from them."[53] His critique of transcendental idealism accords with Bernard Williams's view that a "transcendental, Kantian conception cannot provide any solid foundation for the notions of equality among men, or of equality of respect owed to them."[54]

The original position does not, then, explicitly presuppose our recognizing the "inherent worth and dignity" of persons as rationally autonomous agents. Yet our reflections suggest that only upon the implicit supposition of mutual respect can the original position be defined so that "we get the desired solution."[55] For although Rawls "once says that equality of respect is 'defined' by the first principle of justice," Ronald Dworkin contends that he does "not mean, and in any case he does not argue, that the parties choose to be respected equally in order to advance some more basic right or goal." As Dworkin observes, the "original position is well-designed to enforce the abstract right to equal concern and respect, which must be understood to be the fundamental concept of Rawls's deep theory." Yet if this is so, the right to equal respect cannot be regarded as "a product of the contract" but, rather, appears as "a condition of admission to the original position."[56] For, as Rawls himself concedes, this right is "owed to human beings as moral persons," its origins not resting in the contract but assumed in its design.[57]

The implicit valorization of autonomy in the original position may serve to explain a curious feature of Rawls's account, i.e., his assumption that the principles of justice may be "constructed" by a single rational agent who adopts the perspective of the original position. For within the strictures of the original position, the deliberations of "one person selected at random" would be duly representative.[58]

With actual contracts, consent of a single party is like one hand clapping, yet this merely shows that the ground of compliance is not finally the Hobbesian dictum *"Pacta sunt servanda."* If for Rawls promises derive their moral force (as "constitutive conventions") from the principles of justice, the principles themselves derive their legitimacy from the respect due the "legislative Will" of a rationally autonomous individual.

CONCLUDING REFLECTIONS

Admirable as Rawls's Kantian constructivism might be for political theory or jurisprudence, as moral philosophy it suffers from a certain ambivalence. For, construed procedurally, in terms of the "canons of a reasonable empiricism," the material formulation of the categorical imperative cannot merely be assumed. Nor does Rawls's critique of transcendental idealism permit him to assume that the principles of justice are modally apodictic (synthetic a priori). How, then, are the premises of justice as fairness to be justified *"sub specie aeternitatis,"* in Rawls's words?[59]

Hare is of the mind that Rawls "proceeds, although disclaiming the name, to use appeals to intuition" at the critical junctures of his argument; and indeed, Rawls himself is not averse to describing "justice as fairness" as a "theory of our moral sentiments" as revealed by our "considered judgments in reflective equilibrium."[60] Such judgments are not apodictic in Kant's sense, for the *justificans* of justice as fairness is not its "being true to an order antecedent to . . . us," but, rather, its "congruence with our deeper understanding of ourselves and our aspirations" and our recognition that, in view of our history and traditions, it forms the "most reasonable doctrine for us."[61]

The final justification of the Rawlsian contract rests, then, not in the formal consensus figuring as a regulative ideal in the initial situation but, rather, in "those shared notions and principles thought to be already latent in common sense." Understood in this fashion, the original position is to be regarded not as an "axiomatic (or deductive) basis from which principles are derived" but as a heuristic "thought experiment," permitting us to select those principles "most fitting to the conception of the person" reflected in a modern democratic society.[62]

The formal constraints imposed by Rawls's method of reflective equilibrium have their genesis less in a Kantian "Analytic of Pure Practical Reason" than in an *apologia pro cultura sua*. The objectivity envisioned by Rawls is not the intersubjective validity of Kantian categorical imperatives, for Kantian constructivism regards "moral objectivity" in terms of a "suitably constructed social point of view" congenial to the citizens of a modern democratic society that has attained the requisite degree of wealth. The brevity of Rawls's "eternity" is remarkable, for the latent wisdom imparted to the parties of the original position derives from the "current public views in a well-ordered society."[63]

Kantian constructivism thus resolves itself into a rather respectable form of Humean conventionalism.[64] As Hare's "benevolence" represented a "special and radical" interpretation of universality, so Rawls's implicit valorization of rational autonomy departed from a "pure, procedural" justification of morality. In neither Hare's nor Rawls's analyses did purely formal or procedural considerations suffice to generate a determinate moral theory. For attitudes or motivational assumptions of an antecedently moral nature were tacitly invoked in the material interpretation of universality, be they Hare's benevolence or the dignity of persons as "ends in themselves." Noble as these sentiments may be, it is as yet far from obvious that their provenance is prudence.

NOTES TO CHAPTER 4

1. Wallace Stevens, "Asides on the Oboe," in *The Palm at the End of the Mind*, 187.
2. Hare, "Ethical Theory and Utilitarianism," 25–26; Rawls, *A Theory of Justice*, 51.
3. John Rawls, "Kantian Constructivism in Moral Theory," *Journal of Philosophy* 77, no. 9 (1980): 520, 522, 573.
4. Ibid., 520, 528.
5. Ibid., 523–24.
6. Ibid., 521; cf. John Rawls, *Political Liberalism* (New York: Columbia University Press, 1993), 48, n. 1, 304–7.
7. See Rawls, *A Theory of Justice*, 407–24.
8. Rawls, "Kantian Constructivism in Moral Theory," 525; "Social Unity and Primary Goods," in *Utilitarianism and Beyond*, 164–65.
9. Rawls, "Kantian Constructivism in Moral Theory," 525–26.

10. Ibid., 530.

11. "Rational autonomy" is restricted inasmuch as choice is limited to the primary social goods.

12. Rawls, *A Theory of Justice*, 130–36; "Kantian Constructivism in Moral Theory," 537–39.

13. Rawls, *A Theory of Justice*, 140, 263.

14. Ibid., 126–30.

15. Ibid., 147, 521; cf. *Political Liberalism*, xvi-xviii.

16. Rawls, *A Theory of Justice*, 438. In his later writings, Rawls restricts the scope of his argument to "political" rather than "moral constructivism"; cf. *Political Liberalism*, 89–129.

17. Rawls, *A Theory of Justice*, 140, 188, 255.

18. Rawls, "Social Unity and Primary Goods," 160.

19. Rawls, *Political Liberalism*, xvi; cf. also 36–38.

20. Rawls, "Kantian Constructivism in Moral Theory," 532.

21. *Political Liberalism*, 134. Rawls asserts that "political liberalism supposes that there are many conflicting reasonable doctrines with their conceptions of the good, each compatible with the full rationality of human persons, so far as that can be ascertained with the resources of a political conception of justice." Ibid., 135.

22. Rawls, "Kantian Constructivism in Moral Theory," 532.

23. Rawls, *A Theory of Justice*, 302. Cf. Rawls's most recent revision of the principles in *Political Liberalism* (5–6): "a. Each person has an equal claim to a fully adequate scheme of equal basic rights and liberties, which scheme is compatible with the same scheme for all; and in this scheme the equal political liberties, and only those liberties, are to be guaranteed their fair value. b. Social and economic inequalities are to satisfy two conditions: first they are to be attached to positions and offices open to all under conditions of fair equality of opportunity; and second, they are to be to the greatest benefit of the least advantaged members of society."

24. John Rawls, "A Well-Ordered Society," in *Philosophy, Politics, and Society*, 5th ser., ed. P. Laslett and J. Fishkin (New Haven: Yale University Press, 1979), 18; "The Basic Structure as Subject," *American Philosophical Quarterly* 14 (1977): 165.

25. Kant, *Critique of Practical Reason*, 43.

26. Rawls, *A Theory of Justice*, 51, 255.

27. Ibid., 256.

28. Ibid., 253.

29. Ibid., 92; "Social Unity and Primary Goods," 170; "Kantian Constructivism in Moral Theory," 525–28.

30. Kant, *Groundwork*, 415–16 (42).

31. Rawls, *A Theory of Justice*, 18, 20–21.

32. I understand "prejudice" as it figures in Gadamer's hermeneutical critique, i.e., as a constitutive element of historical understanding; see Gadamer, *Truth and Method*, 265–307.

33. Rawls, *A Theory of Justice*, 125, 127, 137.

34. Ibid., 263.

35. Ibid., 247, 542–43. Cf. *Political Liberalism*, 7.

36. Rawls, "Kantian Constructivism in Moral Theory," 518–19. See likewise Rawls's assertion in *Political Liberalism* (136) that the "background of this question is that, as always, we view citizens as reasonable and rational, as well as free and equal, and we also view the diversity of reasonable religious, philosophical, and moral doctrines found in democratic societies as a permanent feature of their public culture."

37. Michael J. Sandel, *Liberalism and the Limits of Justice* (Cambridge: Cambridge University Press, 1982), 32.

38. Hume, *A Treatise of Human Nature*, (531), 36.

39. Rawls, "Kantian Constructivism in Moral Theory," 527.

40. Thomas Nagel, "Rawls on Justice," in *Reading Rawls*, 9.

41. Ibid.

42. Hare, "Rawls' Theory of Justice," 90; Rawls, *A Theory of Justice*, 183–94.

43. Rawls, *A Theory of Justice*, 175.

44. Rawls, "Kantian Constructivism in Moral Theory," 549–50.

45. Ibid., 527, 550.

46. Ibid., 528. Yet cf. Rawls's assertion in *Political Liberalism* (90, 315–24) that the parties' "highest-order" interest in realizing and developing their moral capacity for fairness (their "sense of justice") is subordinate to their "higher-order" interest in realizing a determinate conception of the good. In Rawls's words, "the parties cannot invoke reasons founded on regarding the development and exercise of this capacity as part of a person's determinate conception of the good." Their hypothetical choice is thus "restricted to reasons founded on regarding it solely as a means to a person's good." Our "sense of justice," that is, does not of itself generate determinate moral (or political) principles.

47. Rawls, "Kantian Constructivism in Moral Theory," 533; cf. also "Social Unity and Primary Goods," 165. In terms of formal logic, the "highest-order" interests of the original contractors generate an intensional context for the description of action, thus limiting the ascription of (intended) actions.

48. Rawls, *A Theory of Justice*, 19, 505–506 (emphasis added).

49. Rawls, "Kantian Constructivism in Moral Theory," 533, 546; "Fairness to Goodness," *Philosophical Review* 84 (1975): 539 (emphasis added).

50. Rawls, *A Theory of Justice*, 179, 586.

51. Ibid., 511 (emphasis added); cf. also Ronald Dworkin, *Taking Rights Seriously* (Cambridge: Harvard University Press, 1978), 150–83.

52. Kant, *Groundwork*, 436–37 (80–81). Cf. Rawls's remark in *A Theory of Justice*, 256: "The principles regulative of the kingdom of ends are those that would be chosen in this position, and the description of this situation enables us to explain the sense in which acting from these principles expresses our nature as free and equal rational persons." Cf. also "Fairness to Goodness," 537; "Kantian Constructivism in Moral Theory," 552.

53. Ibid., 586–87.

54. Bernard Williams, "The Idea of Equality," in *Problems of the Self: Philosophical Papers, 1956–1972* (Cambridge: Cambridge University Press, 1973), 235.

55. Rawls, *A Theory of Justice*, 141.

56. Dworkin, *Taking Rights Seriously*, 181, 272. For Dworkin, the individual liberties elaborated in the social contract find their justification in the equal respect owed rational autonomous agents "who are capable of forming and acting on intelligent conceptions of how their lives should be lived."

57. Ibid., 181; Rawls, *A Theory of Justice*, 504–12.

58. Rawls, *A Theory of Justice*, 139.

59. Ibid., 264, 587.

60. Hare, *Moral Thinking*, 175; "Rawls' Theory of Justice," 87; Rawls, *A Theory of Justice*, 120.

61. Rawls, "Kantian Constructivism in Moral Theory," 519.

62. Ibid., 518, 572.

63. Ibid., 519, 537.

64. Cf. Rawls's favorable comments on Hume in *A Theory of Justice*, 32–33.

PART THREE

Visions and Revisions: Philosophy with a Practical Intent

Our reflections on the Kantian heritage in Part Two set the stage for our critical reconstruction of the concept of *phronēsis* in Part Three. Chapter 5 is devoted to an analysis of the normative implications of rational (prudential) action in light of our earlier criticism of Kantian hypothetical imperatives. Chapter 6 offers a critical assessment of Gadamer's philosophical hermeneutics and, in particular, of his rehabilitation of Aristotelian *phronēsis* for practical philosophy. Our "Concluding Theological Postscript" brings the fruits of our hermeneutical critique of *Moralität* to bear on the vexed question of the distinctiveness of Christian ethics.

5

The Concept of Prudence

"What prize outweighs the priceless worth of prudence?"[1]

SOPHOCLES

With the eclipse of the rich heritage of *phronēsis*, virtue seems but "fragments . . . shored against [our] ruins."[2] A purely formal justification of *Moralität* proved elusive, as our critique revealed Kant's failure to show that the moral law, stipulating the universality of our maxims, could be inferred from the "pure form of law" (i.e., of practical prescription). Indeed, the constructive normative theories of Rawls and Hare finally depended upon their differing interpretations of the "material" formulation of the categorical imperative.

As Kant himself recognized, however, it "is here we encounter the paradox that . . . reverence for a mere idea"—the "mere dignity of humanity"—"should function as an inflexible precept for the will."[3] Villains, says Philippa Foot, are not necessarily imprudent, for "irrational actions are those in which [one] in some way defeats his own purposes, doing what is calculated to be disadvantageous or to frustrate his ends. Immorality does not *necessarily* involve any such thing."[4]

In offering an analytical reconstruction of the idea of prudence, I will argue that the "consistent amoralist" is fittingly censured as imprudent. For if we have "neither behind us nor before us in a luminous realm of values, any means of justification" (in Sartre's words), morality may indeed seem fictive, a "vain illusion" subject to the whims and vagaries of custom.[5] Yet the "mere dignity of humanity" is vindicated not in "pure reason, independently of all experience," as Kant believed, but, rather, in our phronetic "self-knowledge."

Our inquiry commences with (i) a consideration of intentional action description as a prelude to (ii) a critical reconstruction of Kantian hypothetical imperatives of prudence. Our reflections conclude with (iii) an analysis of the moral implications of prudential prescriptions in light of a formal, semantical theory of the good (correlative to phronetic "self-knowledge"). After this interpretation of prudence, chapter 6 will be devoted to a reappraisal of *phronēsis* in Gadamer's philosophical hermeneutics.

INTENTIONAL ACTIONS

The function of "intentional" in my "intention to perform 'A'," is, one might say with Donald Davidson, syncategorematic, generating action descriptions "in terms of their reasons."[6] An action would be fittingly described as "intentional" if it falls under the properties of 'A' that count as my reasons for performing 'A'.[7] Yet, as Davidson recognized in recent writings, merely generating (possible) action descriptions in terms of my pertinent reasons does not suffice to explain the "unconditional judgment" comprising my intention (i.e., the judgment that some action is "more desirable than any available alternative"). The "intentional state" expressed in such judgments bears no "simple relation to the reasons on which it is based," even if these reasons were regarded by the agent as her best reasons, all things considered.[8]

Although the description of intentional actions will be relative to the set of available, pertinent reasons, Davidson concludes that "there is no principle of logic" compelling us to "trim our unconditional judgments of what is best" (i.e., our intentions, so construed) to "our best judgment" (i.e., the judgment conditional upon all "the considerations deemed relevant by the agent").[9] For Davidson, indeed, the incontinent agent acts intentionally, for reason(s) conceived as a conjunct of the set of available, relevant reasons, albeit not for her best reason(s), all things considered.

Intentional action descriptions expressing a "conative propositional attitude," i.e., my judging some action to be more preferable than any available alternative on the basis of my best reasons, or a conjunct of them, may be construed as intensional functions of the form "It is intentional of the practically rational agent 'S', that 'S' does 'A' under the description 'd'."[10] One and the same event, that is, may be depicted as intentional under one description, yet unintentional under another. In the familiar example, it was intentional of Oedipus that he slew the haughty stranger who accosted him on the road from Delphi to Phocis, yet not intentional of Oedipus to have slain his father, the king.[11]

The semantic opacity of action descriptions (where, in Frege's terms, the "reference" of the intended action is specified by the "sense" of the action for Oedipus) implies, then, that only intensionally equivalent descriptions satisfy 'A', e.g., Oedipus's intention to kill the haughty stranger.[12] Yet even such intentional actions may have unintended implications that frustrate our relevant reasons for acting. As the tragedy of Oedipus unfolds, the implications of his action are progressively illumined, giving rise to ever more comprehensive redescriptions of the slaying of the haughty stranger as "the slaying of Laius, the king" and, finally, "the slaying of the king, his father." In the tragic denouement, Sophocles depicts the blind Oedipus as "seeing" what seeing, was blindly done: a fated wisdom, bringing "more misery than [he] can guess." Having fled Corinth lest the Pythian oracle be fulfilled, Oedipus finds that slaying the haughty stranger has unwittingly frustrated "the fair-seeming haven of [his] hopes."[13]

Were one to assume that Oedipus acted rashly in culpable ignorance, his action would fall under the censure of "incontinence" (*akrasia*) as understood by Aristotle. For the incontinent agent acts from "his desire but not from his choice; whereas the continent agent acts from his choice and not from his desire." The incontinent (*akratic*) agent, overwhelmed by nonrational desire (*epithumia*), fails to act in conformity with his rational wish (*boulēsis*) expressed in his "deliberative desire" or choice (*prohairesis*).[14] *Akrasia* is deemed consistent with the doctrine of *eudaimonia*, since reason's minor premise is "a judgment deriving from perception," and it is of "this premise that the incontinent [agent] is prevented by his condition from properly possessing himself. Either that, or, if he does possess it, he does so only in the sense in which possessing does not mean comprehension but only talking, as a drunken man recites the verses of Empedocles."[15] *Akrasia* would not imply, then, what Socrates feared, namely, that knowledge would be "dragged about like a slave." For it is our "aesthetic" perception, not demonstrable knowledge (*epistēmē*), that is obscured by passion.[16]

Although the incontinent action may be represented as the conclusion of a practical syllogism that, per definition, leads "immediately to action," Aristotle refrains from describing the "deliberative desire" of the incontinent agent as choice.[17] Aristotle seems to believe that an agent cannot wittingly apprehend a possible action under the aspect of the good (as a constitutive specification of *eudaimonia*) yet fail, intentionally, to perform it. If, ex hypothesi, one acts intentionally, one's best judgment, reflecting the *hupolepsis* of the good, would necessarily be expressed in one's judgment of what is best (one's intention).

If, however, we accept the modified account of incontinence offered by Davidson, we need not assume that the set of reasons constituting the intentional state of the *eudaimōn* excludes, in principle, a conjunct of this set of reasons from rationalizing action. Oedipus might characterize himself in terms of a general disposition to respect duly constituted authorities, recognize the haughty stranger as such, and yet, under the impetus of desire, wittingly slay him. Oedipus would thus act intentionally, contrary to his own best judgment, without our thereby attributing his *akrasia* to mere ignorance.

Construed in *De Anima* as "a unitary practical conception," *eudaimonia* does not formally exclude the possibility of incontinent actions, since it is a matter of metaphysical, rather than formal, inference that one's "best reason(s)" represent the optimal fulfillment of *all* relevant reasons.[18] The notion of *eudaimonia* as an end "inclusive of all intrinsic goods" (where the *aretai* form a coherent whole), as we have seen, is a metaphysically richer conception than the "truistic" construal of *eudaimonia* as action in accordance with one's best reason(s), all things considered. As David Wiggins argues, forming "a unitary practical conception" of the good need not imply that "there will be no grounds for regret about that which is deemed to be the lesser good." The incontinent agent might thus wittingly choose the smaller good so as to act "for a reason . . . for all that it is a 'bad' reason."[19]

The continent (*enkratic*) agent, conversely, would judge in accordance with "right appetition," so that her best judgment, as expressed in *boulēsis*, is decisive in the formation of her intention. Continence, although not implied as a necessary truth of logic, would form a necessary condition of practically rational agency (while temperance would be its perfection). Even if, following Aristotle, one conceived my intention to perform 'A' as entailed by my "best judgment" in the description of 'A' as that which I have best reason to do, it would still not follow as a mere truth of logic that I *must* form my own best judgment with respect to the "merely possible purposes" attributable to me.

As we shall see, failure to form one's best judgment deprives practical judgments of their requisite exclusivity, while the objective determination of action implies that my intentions be "rationally coherent," i.e., directed to the performance of the action "judged best on the basis of all available relevant reasons." Modeled on Hempel's requirement of "total evidence," Davidson's "principle of continence" is a "directive" the rational agent "will accept." For as the "requirement of total evidence" is not a postulate of a theorem of inductive logic but a "maxim" for its application, so reason is "applied" in the practical realm as the intentions of the practically rational agent are conformed to her best reasons.[20]

HYPOTHETICAL IMPERATIVES

Kant assumed that reason legislated in favor of her practical office, albeit "pathologically," in the formation of hypothetical imperatives. Yet, as our reflections in chapter 2 suggest, a considerable modification of the formal principle of hypothetical imperatives is required if it is to express the "relation of an objective law of reason to a will which is not necessarily determined by this law in virtue of its subjective constitution (the relation of necessitation)."[21] In its Kantian construal, the "objective law" of hypothetical imperatives serves, in Beck's words, as a "tacit premise or rule of practical inference," distinguished from all mere subjective maxims. As Kant formulates it, "Who wills the end, wills (so far as reason has decisive influence on his actions) also the means which are indispensably necessary and in his power."[22] The logical transfer of desire, of "willing an end" (as "an effect possible in a certain way through me"), to my "willing the requisite, possible means" (my "acting in the same way with respect to it"), conveys no novel information regarding the cognitive content of my reasons. For Kant, the formal principle of hypothetical imperatives, whether assertoric or problematic in modality, is "so far as willing is concerned . . . analytic."[23]

Kant's restriction of ends to the representation of sensuous inclination, directed to the "production" of an effect not itself an action, is, as we have seen, unduly restrictive, as is his reduction of prudential imperatives to mere *consilia*. And even graver lacunae appear in his account, for the formal principle of hypothetical imperatives does not as yet suffice to show how action is objectively determined. Construing "willing an end" as a complex concept implying "willing (necessarily if one accords with reason) the sole means which are in one's power" merely generates an action description in terms of a pertinent "desirability characteristic" (in Anscombe's phrase), i.e., 'A' as a means through which one of many "merely possible purposes" might be realized. The desirability characteristic of serving as a means to my end would constitute a reason for acting *if* I will the end, so that 'A' is described in terms of a "merely possible" or "prima facie" reason for acting.

As we have seen, the semantic opacity of intentional action descriptions implies that an action may be variously characterized with respect to the reasons that rationalize it. 'A' may reflect a certain desirability characteristic under description 'd' but another desirability characteristic under description 'd_1'. Since the formal coherence of "willing an end" and "willing the requisite possible means" is not defined by reference to a particular (cognitively specified) event, one cannot infer from mere analysis of the event intended under the aspect of "means" what other pertinent desirability characteristics it might display. The action description generated by reference to a discrete end might thus be logically independent of the description generated by another end, even though the descriptions be satisfied by a single, possible event.

Analysis of discrete ends may rationalize, or fail to rationalize, the same event, so that Oedipus might have reason to slay the haughty stranger under one description yet have even greater reason to refrain from slaying him under another. For Oedipus's intention to slay the haughty stranger would not imply his forsaking his intention to elude the prophecy's fulfillment, even though his intentions are, de facto, existentially exclusive. My choice to embark upon the course of action necessary for achieving one end need not, then, *necessarily* entail my forsaking other ends that would be frustrated were I to succeed.[24] My ends may unwittingly conflict, as when Oedipus misconstrues his desire to discover the killer of Laius as a means to vindicate himself before the Theban populace.

Prudence, we might say, supplies the requisite wit. For if, as a rational being, I am "concerned with desires" (as prima facie reasons), which in their evaluative comparison suffice for the objective determination of action, it seems reasonable to believe that I will act in accordance with my "greatest" or "best reason(s)," all things considered. Assuming that reason is truly "practical in its own right" implies the possibility of generating action descriptions representing my relevant reasons for acting in light of their relative deliberative priority, a determination of which pertinent prima facie reasons will be decisive. (Such an evaluative comparison merely implies that my pertinent attitudes and beliefs suffice for the determination of my best reason[s]; one need not assume the reductive or nonreductive commensuration of values as in the case of pleasure or utility, respectively.)[25]

Inasmuch as the practically exclusive sense of "ought" (*Sollen*) implies that it cannot be the case that under one description I "ought" to do 'A' but under another I "ought" not, the conclusion of the apodosis (that I "ought" to perform 'A') presumes that no further pertinent reasons tell decisively against my performing 'A'.[26] The protasis of the Kantian conditional ("if one wills an end") would accordingly be subject to the further qualification "if one's end satisfies one's best judgment, conditional upon all pertinent considerations." The action description figuring in the apodosis is generated through a consideration of the pertinent primary and secondary reasons (a formal, analytical relation obtaining between the conception of the pertinent reasons rationalizing 'A' in the protasis, i.e., the ends "possible in a certain way through me," and the primary reason that characterizes 'A' in the apodosis, i.e., the description of 'A' as satisfying my pertinent secondary reasons).

Amended thus, the formal principle of hypothetical imperatives implies that a rational agent will act in accordance with her best reason(s), all things considered, and "ought" to do so if tempted otherwise. Hypothetical imperatives govern my intentions, so that the logical nexus of "acting in accordance with my best reason(s)" and my intention is provided by the tacit condition "so far as reason has decisive influence on my actions."[27] The formal principle, that is, must be conceived as a rule not merely of practical inference but of my acting.

Were we a race of perfectly incontinent agents, the antipodes of Kant's perfectly rational or holy beings, our best judgments would invariably fail to determine our actions. It would not suffice, then, merely that I have a reason for acting, as in the Kantian formulation of "willing a means," nor that 'A' is fittingly described as that which I have best reason(s) to do. It must likewise be the case that "what I do" as a practically rational agent concerned with desires is explicated in terms of my disposition to regard my best judgment as decisive in forming my intentions. For only insofar as I prescribe *unconditionally*

that I act in accordance with my best reason(s) would my best judgment conditional upon all relevant considerations, suffice for the objective determination of my intention, i.e., the unconditional judgment that this course of action is to be preferred to other available
alternatives. That I so prescribe is not to be inferred from some more
primitive premise but is, rather, in the words of Wittgenstein, "simply
what I do" as a practically rational agent, subject to inclination.[28]

As our earlier reflections suggest, intimations of this more comprehensive principle are present in Kant's analysis of hypothetical
(assertoric) imperatives of prudence, to which problematic imperatives
of skill are assimilated in the *Critique of Practical Reason*.[29] But while
for Kant prudential imperatives lack the force of objective law, our
analysis reveals that it is prudence, once purified of its conceptual
obscurity, that displays reason's practical office. Our consideration
of the formal principle of hypothetical imperatives presumes what
Davidson terms the "principle of continence," which stipulates that
I "perform the action judged best on the basis of all available relevant
reasons."[30] Yet the formal requirement of prudence incorporates an
aspect of Aristotle's analysis not fully explicated by Davidson. For
Aristotle assumes not merely that the continent agent will act in accordance with her best judgment but that her best judgment will reflect
"right appetition." My best judgment must thus be suitably formed in
light of the available, relevant reasons (as we shall see in the following
section, this implies that my best judgment honors the pertinent semantic constraints upon my conception of the good). For Aristotle,
"folly [in formulating one's best judgment] combined with incontinence" is not a virtue, as the Sophists alleged, for "although it may
be "incidentally by any choice, it is essentially by the *true* principle and
the right choice that the [continent agent] abides, and the [incontinent
agent] does not."[31]

PRACTICAL PRESCRIPTION

It is as imperfectly rational agents, says Kant, that we are subject
to practically rational prescription. "Ought" occurs in its practically
rational sense in judgments prescribing that a practically rational agent
'S' act in accordance with her best reason(s), all things considered.
Formally, "ought" figures as a propositional operator signifying that
it be the case "that 'p'," where 'p' is satisfied by the intentional action

description "'S' performs 'A' under the description 'd.'" If, then, 'A' is fittingly described as that which 'S' has best reason(s) to do, all things considered, then 'S' ought to do 'A' under the pertinent description.

The Objectivity of Practical Prescription

'S's performing 'A' under the pertinent description is, in Kantian terms, "objectively necessary" yet "subjectively contingent." The formal principle is thus "practically necessitating" for imperfect rational agents. If we (qua practically rational prescribers) differ as to whether 'S_1' ought to perform 'A' under the description 'd', we differ with respect to whether 'A' is fittingly described as that which 'S_1' has best reason(s) to do, not with respect to whether, *if* 'A' is fittingly described, 'S_1' ought to perform it.

The Universality of Practical Prescription

The formal principle, so construed, is universally quantified for 'S' inasmuch as the explication of the prescription that a practically rational agent 'S' ought to act in accordance with her best reason(s), all things considered, implies neither proper names, individual constants, nor indexical terms. The objective (intersubjective) validity of the prescription is unaffected by the mere numerical distinction of agents, although such distinction may, of course, be semantically relevant in the (logically) subsequent interpretation of my best reason(s). One thus prescribes for the domain of imperfect "rational beings in general" that "'S' perform 'A' under the description 'd'," where 'd' is explicated in terms of 'S's best reason(s), all things considered.

Judgments of the Form 'O(p)'

As our practical judgments do not descend from the empyrean, we might assume that the sense of a locution such as "'S' ought to perform 'A' under the description 'd'" is relative to the conditions under which it may be regarded as "true" or objectively valid for a representative rational prescriber such as myself. We shall consider the implications of construing the "objectivity" of practical judgments in accordance with Tarski's "Convention 'T'.") In practical judgments, reason, says Kant, is directed to its object not "merely in determining it and its concept" (as in theoretical judgments) but in "making it real."[32] Such judgments might thus be conceived as expressing a conative propositional attitude with respect to the intentional action description signified by 'p', i.e., my pro attitude, or interest qua 'S', "that 'p'." In judging that "'S$_1$' ought to perform 'A' under the description 'd'," I prescribe implicitly that 'S$_1$'s intention be "rationally coherent" inasmuch as it expresses her best judgment, all things considered.

"Ought" in its practically rational sense thus governs the formation of 'S$_1$'s intentions, expressing, in Kantian terms, the "interest" of reason in 'S' ("rational beings in general") forming rationally coherent intentions, i.e., of 'S' forming and acting in accordance with 'S's best judgment.[33] Yet the interest of reason in 'S's forming rationally coherent intentions cannot be regarded as a "further" reason informing 'S's best judgment, lest 'S's action be regressively defined in terms of the thought that 'S' ought to perform it. Reason's interest is rather logically antecedent to the semantical interpretation of 'A', prescribing for, in Kant's terms, "a certain setting of the will to act from a certain motive," i.e., to act from one's best reason(s).

As in Lewis Carroll's delightful tale "Achilles and the Tortoise" Achilles must assume *modus ponens* in seeking to justify it (since, as Hare remarks, "this is the rule that gives its meaning to 'if'"), so the formal principle of hypothetical imperatives (suitably reconstructed) is exhibited in our rational prescriptions as "the ultimate guide to action."[34] The formal principle, analytically explicating the practical sense of "ought," is tautological yet not, for that reason, in Wittgenstein's term, "nonsensical" (*unsinnig*). For it illumines the context of rational action, "showing forth" reason's pure, practical interest in action, my interest, that is, that 'S' (qua "rational being") act in accordance with her best reason(s), all things considered. It would, conversely, be "nonsensical" for perfectly intemperate agents who, lacking such an interest, might confess that "I ought to do 'A' under the description 'd'" yet blithely do otherwise.

One may thus obey, as Wittgenstein says, "blindly," yet not "without reason," for although the description of an action in terms of my best reason(s) implies my belief that there is no further, available pertinent reason, one has not thereby reached an *aporia* in which reasons have ceased to figure.[35] Rather, reason's pure, practical interest in action implies that one's best reason(s) *suffices* for the determination of action. One's best reason(s) would be, for the prudential agent, of decisive influence in the formation of her intentions.

Rational Autonomy

The conative propositional attitude exhibited in judgments of the form 'O(p)' is logically independent of my empirical locution 'O(p)' but not of reason's pure interest, of which it is the concrete expression. For reason's interest is exhibited in the ideally regulative status of the formal principle "as a guide to action."[36] The formal explication of the syntax of judgments of the form 'O(p)' presumes that "what we do" in rationally prescribing is exhibit reason's pure, practical interest in 'S' (whether myself or another) forming and acting in accordance with her best judgment, i.e., in 'S' acting autonomously.

As we have seen, the sense of a locution such as "'S_1' ought to perform 'A' under the description 'd'" is relative to the conditions under which it may be regarded as true, or objectively valid for "practically rational agents in general." One could not, consistent with the objectivity of practical prescriptions, say that it is true for 'S_1' that "'S_1' ought to perform 'A' under the pertinent description" yet not "true for us," i.e., that 'S_1' ought to perform 'A' so described. Conversely, if it is true that 'S_1' ought to perform 'A' under the description 'd', and assuming the domain of 'S' forms a subset of rational prescribers, then it is implicitly true for 'S_1' that this is so. The objectivity and universality of practical judgments, coupled with the assumption that the domain of 'S' comprises a subset of rational prescribers, permits us to assume that 'S_1' prescribes reflectively for the domain of 'S', i.e., that for any representative rational agent 'S_1', it is true that the intentions of 'S_1, S_2, S_3, . . . S_n' ought to be rationally coherent.

If, then, 'S_1' ought to perform 'A' under the description 'd', as the subject of hypothetical imperatives, it is likewise the case that 'S_1' is capable of being represented as their author. In Kant's terms, we might say that "the will is therefore not merely subject to the law, but is so subject that it must be considered as also making the law for itself, and precisely on this account as first of all subject to the law (of which it can regard itself as the author)."[37] Following Rawls, we might say that actions in accordance with hypothetical imperatives express our "rational autonomy"; and indeed, our critique of Kantian *Moralität* revealed that autonomy, as the "fact of pure reason," may be thus construed. (In chapter 2, our analysis of categorical imperatives showed that reason exercises its practical office through our "autonomous" prescriptions of the form 'O(p).') Actions, conversely, would be "heteronomous" inasmuch as they fail to correspond to our rationally coherent intentions as the object of practical prescription.

One need not suppose that rationally autonomous action is necessarily accompanied by the explicit thought that I ought to perform it; it suffices for my subjection to the formal principle of hypothetical imperatives that I exhibit the pertinent interest in the "condition of rational willing" expressed "in a certain setting of the will to act from a certain motive," i.e., from my best reason(s), all things considered. My actions thus proceed from a will in accordance with reason, so that the judgment "I ought to do 'A' under the relevant description" might be fittingly imputed to me.

Reason's Pure, Practical Interest

Prescriptions of the form 'O(p)' show forth reason's pure, practical interest (universally distributed for 'S') in 'S' forming and acting in accordance with her best reason(s), i.e., in 'S' acting "autonomously." "Autonomy" signifies the condition under which a practical prescription is true for me qua 'S', for I am subject to practical prescriptions precisely as I exhibit reason's pure, practical interest. Qua 'S', I prescribe from the perspective of a formally generalized interest in rationally autonomous actions, so that my intentional state is bounded, as it were, by an "interest" in virtue of which "reason becomes practical—that is, becomes a cause determining the will."[38] Yet though our definition of interest harks back to Kant, our entitlement to assume reason's pure interest is far less obscure. For Kant, the "pure, practical interest" of reason in determining moral action remains "incomprehensible," for one must assume that "a mere thought containing nothing sensible in itself" (i.e., pure idea of will) can "determine sensibility in accordance with rational principles."[39] The perplexity, as we remarked, extends no less to the formation of Kantian hypothetical imperatives, for their formal principle is likewise a priori and objectively necessitating, independent of the synthetic a posteriori determination of the merely possible purposes over which it ranges. (As we have seen, moral and prudential imperatives represent semantical interpretations of the pure form of law 'O(p),' as the formal expression of reason's pure, practical interest.)

The incomprehensibility of reason's pure, practical interest is, of course, vexing only if we assume with Kant that "a defense" is required of an "interest," which, although itself prior to all experience, suffices to determine sensibility in accordance with rational principles.[40] Our present construal, however, commits us only to the assumption that reason is practical, defining a form of *experience* characterized by the expression of our "self-knowledge" (qua 'S'), i.e., our "knowledge of the good" as specified by reason's pure, practical interest in 'S' forming and acting (autonomously) in accordance with her best reason(s), all things considered.

In Kantian language, the "self-consciousness of a pure practical reason" is explicated in terms of reason's pure interest, as our self-knowledge is displayed in practical prescription. Here one might say with Wittgenstein that "we have reached bedrock" and no further explanation or defense is possible.[41] Indeed, the status of the formal principle of hypothetical imperatives is not unlike that of the formally necessary truths of logic in Wittgenstein's analysis. Functions defined by logical stipulation are formally tautological or true by virtue of their logical form regardless of the truth values of their constitutive variables. "The propositions of logic are tautologies," writes Wittgenstein in the *Tractatus*. "Therefore the propositions of logic say nothing. (They are the analytic propositions.)" In the analysis of such propositions, "[o]ne can recognize that they are true from the symbol alone."[42] Yet while lacking sense ("*sinnlos*"), logical truths are not finally nonsensical ("*unsinnig*") for, although possessing no subject matter, they elucidate "the logical form of reality," showing "what cannot be said."[43]

The regulative status of formally necessary logical propositions is displayed in language. As one's reasoning is expressed in well-formed propositions, so any explication of the truths of logic must reflectively exhibit them. It would thus be illusory to imagine a celestial (extralinguistic) perspective from which one could intelligibly inquire whether the truths of logic admit of semantical justification, as if they could be informatively compared with that which they disclose. As tautologies, they illumine what is "true" for us.

In Wittgenstein's later writing, analytical, a priori "grammatical utterances" show forth "our acting which lies at the bottom of the language-game," rather than the "logical form of reality" as presupposed in the metaphysical atomism of the *Tractatus*.[44] For, in the words of Wittgenstein, "in the end, logic cannot be described. You must look at the practice of language, then you will see it."[45] The limits of language are finally limits of, and not "in," *our* world, so that the grammatical utterances can be shown or reflectively explicated from within the language in which they figure, but not demonstrably justified.

As *modus ponens* was "shown forth" in Achilles' linguistic "practice," so the formal premise of practical inference, though not itself a necessary truth of logic, illumines what is "true for us" in the "knowledge situation" of practical reason. One need not, then, assume that the formal principle may be justified "independently of all experience," as if the formal rule of *Wille* descended from the empyrean upon a feckless *Willkür*. For in the practical language game, my "self-knowledge" is expressed in my practically rational interest, formally generalized for 'S', in 'S$_1$, S$_2$, S$_3$, . . . S$_n$' forming rationally coherent intentions.

Normative Implications

The self-knowledge of the *phronimos*, so construed, remains relative to the domain of 'S', for my interest in rationally autonomous action is logically prior to the interpretation of *my* reasons for acting. Reason's pure, practical interest thus forms an intensional context for the interpretation of my reasons, so that, qua 'S', *my* best reasons are implicitly delimited by my formally generalized interest in rationally autonomous behavior. My reasons as a rationally autonomous subject are informed by my interest denominating me as an autonomous author, without thereby assuming that reason's interest in rational action is itself yet a further reason for acting. (As we have seen, reason's interest shows, rather than says, that one's best reasons suffice for the objective determination of action, forming the "aesthetic" context of deliberation.)

My belief that 'A' is fittingly described as that which 'S$_1$' has best reason(s) to do (whether I be subject or author of the prescription) thus presumes not only the intentional coherence of the beliefs and attitudes forming 'S$_1$'s best reason(s) but the coherence of these "merely possible purposes" with the pure, practical interest attributed to 'S' as such. The mere occurrence of sensuous inclination would not suffice for the relevant rationalization of my actions, for, contrary to Hobbes's memorable assertion, the thoughts of practical reason are not merely to "the Desires, as Scouts and Spies, to range abroad, and find the way to the things Desired."[46] For the things desired must themselves be consistent with "what I do" as a rationally autonomous agent in prescribing reflectively for the domain of 'S', i.e., with what Aristotle describes as the *phronimos*'s "knowledge of the good for oneself," or one's "self-knowledge."

The set of beliefs and attitudes forming my best reason(s) must reflect my status as a rationally autonomous agent, so that the generation of intentional action descriptions satisfying 'p' in my prescriptions (of the form 'O(p)') is consistent with the possibility of *my* acting autonomously. Just as Kant believed one's maxims must be consistent with the possibility of their being willed as universal law (in view of the "constitutive" sense of universality, as constituting one's sole motive), so my reasons must be consistent with the reflective exhibition of autonomy as I prescribe from the perspective of a "rational being in general."

My reasons, qua 'S', will thus reflect my respect for the rational autonomy of agents. For my interest, qua 'S', is directed not to the performance of a particular (cognitively specified) event *per se* but, rather, to the occurrence of actions fittingly described as rationally autonomous. In Kantian terms, reason's pure interest in action, expressed in the conative propositional attitude of judgments of the form 'O(p)', governs the formal determination of volitions, so that autonomous actions exhibit our "rational nature," a nature that Kant says is not "produced" but reflectively disclosed in action.[47]

The "self-consciousness" of a pure practical reason, exhibited in my practical prescriptions, determines my will so as to impart to the sensuous world "the form of a system of rational beings."[48] In so legislating reflectively for the "disclosedness" (*alētheia*) of rational nature, one prescribes implicitly for a kingdom of ends. Indeed, the ideal of a "moral commonwealth" forms, as it were, the objective correlative of my "self-knowledge" as *phronimos*, adumbrating a formal semantics of the good, i.e., the evaluative perspective within which my reasons are interpreted.[49]

In terms reminiscent of Kant's formulation of the categorical imperative, we might argue that my pure, practical interest in the generation of rationally coherent (autonomous) actions presumes (i) formally, the compossibility of objectively prescribed actions, (ii) materially, the ideal of respect for rational nature as an end in itself, and (iii), as a complete determination of practical prescription, the convergence of practical judgments in attaining a kingdom of ends.

The Formal Determination Reason's pure interest in the formation of rationally coherent intentions (of intentions expressing 'S's best reason[s]) recurs, as we have seen, in the description of 'S' as a rationally *autonomous* agent. *My* rationally coherent intentions (fittingly predicated of me as an autonomous agent) will thus reflect my respect for the rationally coherent intentions of others. Since, *mutatis mutandis*, this is true of all 'S', our rationally coherent intentions will themselves form a coherent whole, exhibiting "a harmony or coherence of rational wills."[50]

We might, then, concur with Kant that "[e]very action is just (right) that in itself or in its maxim is such that the freedom of the will, i.e., the autonomy, of each can coexist together with the freedom of everyone in accordance with a universal law."[51] Yet we need not suppose that the "universal law" of *impartial* respect (in attaining a harmony of subjective ends) emulates the "universal uniformity" of natural, empirical laws. For we may differ "respectfully" in our maxims and intentions, provided our intentional actions are compossible, so constituting a possible kingdom of ends.

Alluding to the analysis of H. J. Paton, Beck observes that, for Kant, the "order of nature under [universal] law" implies not only a "uniform sequence of phenomena under causal law" but likewise the "organic" coherence of natural purposes, which serves only as an ideal methodological assumption in reason's seeking a totality of conditions.[52] The teleological ideal of nature as a harmonious totality serves, by analogy, in the moral realm as a regulative idea for practice, so that, as a wise creator of the moral order, one would prescribe for the harmonious realization of subjective ends.

Although only the latter conception of universality is implied by our reflections, it suffices for the refutation of MacIntyre's contention that one could consistently *"will* a universe of egoists," all of whom abide by the maxim "Let 'everyone except me be treated as a means.'"[53] For a series of mutually exclusive singular prescriptions would be generated that imply that it both be and not be the case that '$S_1, S_2, S_3 \ldots S_n$' be treated as a means and not at the same time as an end. In a "universe of egoists," each egoist would be excepted and included in one's willing. Even were such a fissiparous universe imaginable, it could not consistently be willed as the outcome of prudential prescription.[54]

The Material Determination Inasmuch as my obedience to hypothetical imperatives presupposes my autonomy, my reasons will reflect the condition under which a rational prescription can objectively determine action, i.e., my "interest" in the reflective exhibition of 'S' as rationally autonomous. Forming the intensional context of the interpretation of my reasons (in Kant's terms, my subjective ends), the pure, practical interest of reason is fulfilled in the exhibition (the *alētheia*, or "practical truth") of rationally autonomous action, i.e., in our attaining a kingdom of ends.

Since my interest is formally generalized for 'S' (my interest in autonomous behavior being logically prior to the numerical distinction of agents' reasons), my self-consciousness as a rationally autonomous agent reflects my "citizenship" in a kingdom of ends. I am, indeed, entitled to regard myself as an "end," precisely as the "self-knowledge" exhibited in my prescription discloses my membership in such a realm. In prescribing reflectively for the domain of 'S', I "show forth" myself as a "self-existent" (*selbständiger*) end (whose normative status is formally antecedent to the producible ends distinguishing agents).[55]

As we have seen in Ronald Dworkin's criticism, such an understanding of "equal respect" for rational agents, "capable of forming and acting on intelligent conceptions of how their lives should be lived," is tacitly assumed in Rawls's "deep theory."[56] Impartial respect for the "positive" aspect of freedom as autonomy, i.e., for the "highest-order" interests of moral subjects, is presumed in the design of the original position. Finally, Rawls's rational choosers are not inspired merely by rational self-love, for the relevant sense of *my* in "my best reason(s)" reflects my status as a rationally autonomous subject of a kingdom of ends. The *phronimos*, even in modern guise, is not a bare ascriptive subject of desire for whom morality is the *poiēsis* of a supreme fiction.

The Complete Determination As we have seen, the teleological conception of a kingdom of ends serves as an a priori regulative ideal of reason in offering a complete account of objectively determined actions. For moral *teleology*, accordingly, the notion of a "possible kingdom of ends as a kingdom of nature" serves as "a practical Idea used to bring into existence what . . . can be made actual by our conduct—and indeed to bring it into existence in conformity with this Idea."[57] Since the *telos* of rational prescription is not a producible state of affairs but, rather, the reflective exhibition of the "intelligible personality," moral teleology describes our autonomous "self-mediation," i.e., the realization, through our conduct, of a possible kingdom of ends. As in Aristotle's ethics, "self-knowledge" and "knowledge of the good for oneself" are mutually implicatory as one's rational autonomy is displayed in legislating for a moral commonwealth in which "humanity in one's own person is regarded as holy."[58]

CONCLUDING REFLECTIONS

In these pages, I have sought to show that a theory of morality founded upon prudence need not be a "vain illusion and splendid misery." Indeed, the various formulae of the categorical imperative, if suitably emended, may be represented as the internal fruition of prudence. One modern theorist of note, Alan Gewirth, has argued in a like vein, and a comparison of his ethical rationalism with the foregoing account of moral teleology commends itself.

While I argue that our "self-knowledge" (and hence "self-interest") is tempered by the regulative ideal of a kingdom of ends, Gewirth proceeds from the "dialectically necessary" prerequisites of "prospective, purposive agency." In *Reason and Morality*, Gewirth assumes that informed, rational (prudential) choice presupposes our regarding freedom and well-being, the "necessary conditions" of our "pursuit of purposes," as "necessary goods."[59] Such goods are deemed rights by the agent, yet Gewirth does not thereby merely assume the principle of equal respect as the foundation of his "deep theory." Nor, as in utilitarian analysis, must we assume the interpersonal comparison of our various purposes. For the other-regarding aspects of rights' theory are derived from the prudential self-regard of our rational agent.

One commences from the prudential perspective of what Rawls termed our "higher-order" interest in "protecting and advancing" one's conception of the good, rather than from a tacit regard for the "highest-order" interests of moral persons as rationally autonomous agents. Formal considerations, recalling the first formulation of the categorical imperative (in its regulative construal) are introduced as sufficient reason for generalizing the initial ascription of rights' claims. The "non-moral," prudential "ought" acquires moral (universal) import since, to "avoid self-contradiction," I must admit that the "generic rights" presumed for the exercise of my prospective, purposive agency must be accorded all prospective, purposive agents. I must, then, "refrain from interfering with [my] recipients' freedom and well-being," acting in accordance with their "generic rights" as well as my own.[60]

The "canonical form" in which Gewirth's reasoning is expressed is the "precept addressed to every agent: Act in accord with the generic rights of your recipients as well as of yourself." Termed the "Principle of Generic Consistency," the precept combines "the formal consideration of consistency" with the "material consideration of rights to the generic features or goods of action," as specified by the agent's freedom and well-being. For Gewirth, these generic features, viewed as the "most general and proximate necessary conditions" of purposive activity, offer "objective, ineluctable contents for testing the truth or correctness of moral judgments." The generic features of action are not "correspondence correlates" of moral judgments but, rather, establish, through "the normative structure of action, certain requirements for moral judgments," thus serving as "necessary premises from which moral judgments logically follow."[61]

While Hare and Rawls subject the singular prescriptions of prudence to the formal constraints of moral choice, Gewirth contends that an analysis of such prescriptions suffices for the extension of generic rights to all prospective, purposive agents. Yet as the indexical distinction of the reasons of $'S_1, S_2, S_3, \ldots S_n'$ remains a relevant consideration, the assumption that every purposive agent must respect *her* freedom and well-being cannot be regarded as tantamount to the assumption that every purposive agent must respect the generic rights of agents (sans subscript). For singular prescriptions may be properly attributed to every agent, i.e., universally distributed, without thereby implying the universal prescription that "humanity in one's own person" (qua prospective, purposive agent) be respected.

As Kant recognized (and assuming the Humean circumstances of justice), such a universalization of prudence results not in a universal teleology wherein "universal happiness" is a "type of the morally good" but, rather, in an intermonadic universe of competing subjective ends, "the extreme opposite of harmony, the most arrant conflict."[62] In the words of R. M. Hare, it would indeed be perfectly consistent to admit to being a purposive agent—so that one is "bound to assent to *singular* prescriptions, and even to claim rights" in a weak, nonuniversalizable sense—while refraining from prescribing universally, i.e., "claiming rights in the strong, universalizable sense," which compels one to "accord them to others too."[63]

Even were we to concede the obligation of a prospective, purposive agent to desire a state of affairs in which her freedom and well-being were universally respected, her desire would not suffice to justify her honoring the like claims of others, or their honoring hers.

Autonomous agents might advance certain claims as prospective, purposive agents without assuming that the "fact" of autonomous agency
(the *quaestio facti* of autonomy) suffices for their justification. In Gewirth's construal, indeed, autonomy functions in a merely regulative
sense, inasmuch as my putative rights' claims finally derive their force
from the "various purposes" I pursue (reflecting my "higher-order"
interest), rather than from the regulative ideal of autonomous agents
as ends in themselves.

Although, as Gewirth says, freedom and well-being are "necessary conditions" of my "pursuit of purposes," my desire of the "necessary goods" will be a function of the particular purposes I pursue,
rather than of the "pursuit of purposes," which serves only as a middle
term in the argument. The evaluative construal of the conditions of
agency will be relative to my particular subjective ends and not to
the a priori valorization of "pursuing purposes." In Kantian terms,
autonomous agency will thus have a "price," rather than a "dignity,"
and one has no assurance that its price will not fluctuate with the
relative intensity and duration of one's purposes.[64] One cannot merely
assume a single estimation to prevail, nor is one assured that the
instrumental value accorded the generic features of action is of sufficient "weightiness" to qualify them as rights. Might one not, indeed,
envision circumstances in which one's conception of well-being dimin-
ishes the relative significance of certain liberties cherished in Gewirth's
panoply of rights?[65]

Yet if, as envisaged in these pages, the rational autonomy of
agents is reflectively disclosed in our prescriptions as an object of
reverence, "rational nature" appears as an end in itself. The apriority
of reason's pure, practical interest with respect to all merely possible
purposes provides for the generation of action descriptions exhibiting
one's status as a subject member of a moral commonwealth. Mere
self-interest would be neither formally generalized, as in Gewirth's
ethical rationalism, nor subject to extrinsic, formal constraints, as in
the hypothetical choice theories of Hare and Rawls. For my interest
or pro attitude respecting rationally autonomous behavior generates
an intensional context in which my "self-knowledge" limits the reasons fittingly attributed to me.

If my self-reflection qua 'S' thus exhibits "humanity in myself" as
the "aesthetic" context of interpreting my reasons, I will seek maxims
consistent with attaining a kingdom of ends. As elaborated in our
reconstruction of the various formulae of the categorical imperative,

the regulative ideal of "humanity in my own person" serves as a reflective, teleological delimitation of my intentions, as my *eupraxia* exhibits reason's pure, practical interest in the harmonious realization of a kingdom of ends.

Yet the regulative ideal of respect for persons cannot be regarded as a supreme deductive principle from which the individual *casus* may be unproblematically inferred. For the ideal assumes a regulative status only relative to agents' intentions, reflecting their particular beliefs and attitudes, their immediate apprehension of the circumstances of action. The ideal of respect thus informs the aesthetic context of our perceiving the "ultimate particular" in terms of which my general maxims are concretely specified.[66]

As the kingdom of ends forms the aesthetic context of my deliberation, my *eupraxia* instantiates "humanity in myself" as a *universale concretum*. In harmonizing with a possible kingdom of ends, my maxims will seek to express "a systematic union of rational beings under common objective laws—that is, a kingdom." One envisions a "whole of all ends in systematic conjunction (a whole both of rational beings as ends in themselves and also of the personal ends which each may set before himself)."[67] For, even prior to their material interpretation, the set of possible ends attributable to me qua 'S' presumes the moral order of interacting wills.

Although our maxims need not emulate the "universal uniformity" of nature's laws, they will define a possible world as a kingdom of ends. The set of objectively determined actions instantiating such a kingdom must be coherently specified. Should our maxims prove to be exclusive, our prima facie reasons would not as yet suffice for the objective determination of action; deliberation would proceed until an implicit consensus is attained respecting "rational beings as ends in themselves and . . . the personal ends" which each affected agent may set before herself.[68]

The ideal of rational consensus as the *telos* of practical discourse must be complemented with an analysis of the implicit normative constraints defining its "contours." For certain maxims may satisfy the more stringent Kantian formulation of the moral law. Such maxims would be predicated upon a recognition of the conditions of the possibility of our exercising rationally autonomous agency. Assuming, for instance, that a modicum of liberty, physical security, or nutritional well-being is deemed prerequisite for our *eupraxia*, a practically rational agent would be entitled to claim that other agents respect her civil-political liberties, refrain from doing her bodily or psychological harm, and honor her subsistence rights. Since such claims are a function not merely of the particular purposes I happen to pursue but, rather, of my fittingness to pursue them as a rationally autonomous agent, they may be accorded the status of a right, implicitly extended to the domain of 'S'.

One might, indeed, proceed to construct a theory of rights in the fashion indicated by Gewirth (i.e., in terms of the "generic goods" of freedom and well-being), once the principle of equal respect is assured.[69] Such a theory, derived not from prudential self-regard but, rather, from our self-knowledge as citizens of a moral commonwealth, would permit us to identify and redress what Habermas terms the "systematic distortions" of our communicative interaction, i.e., illusory or coerced consensus.[70] And though we can but adumbrate it now, a phronetic theory of rights, as we shall see in chapter 6, defines a via media between the abstract formalism of Kantian *Moralität* and ethical (*sittlich*) interpretations of the common good.

NOTES TO CHAPTER 5

1. Sophocles *Antigone*, line 1051, p. 154.

2. Eliot, "The Waste Land," line 431, p. 50.

3. Kant, *Groundwork*, 439 (85).

4. Philippa Foot, "Morality as a System of Hypothetical Imperatives," 161–62.

5. Jean-Paul Sartre, *Existentialism and Humanism*, trans. Philip Mairet (London: Methuen, 1948), 33–34, 55–56.

6. Davidson, *Essays on Actions and Events*, 8.

7. These reasons may be distinguished in terms of their immediacy to the action thereby rationalized. The "primary reason" for performing 'A', assuming 'A' is performed intentionally, consists, in Davidson's words, of "a pro attitude of the agent towards actions with a certain property and a belief of the agent that 'A', under the description 'd', has that property." My "secondary reasons" consist of the pertinent attitudes and beliefs that "verify, vindicate, or support" my primary reason. Cf. Davidson, *Essays on Actions and Events*, 5, 8.

8. Donald Davidson, "Reply to Essays I–X," in *Essays on Davidson: Actions and Events*, ed. Bruce Vermazen and Merrill B. Hintikka (Oxford: Oxford University Press, 1985), 196–97.

9. Ibid., 201.

10. Ibid., 206; *Essays on Actions and Events*, 25.

11. Cf. Martha Kneale and William Kneale, *The Development of Logic* (Oxford: Clarendon Press, 1962), 609.

12. Gottlob Frege, "On Sense and Meaning," in *Translations from the Philosophical Writings of Gottlob Frege,* ed. Peter Geach and Max Black, 3d ed. (Oxford: Basil Blackwell, 1980), 56–78.

13. Sophocles *King Oedipus,* in *The Theban Plays,* lines 420–28, p. 37.

14. Aristotle *Nicomachean Ethics* 1111b13–15, 1148a9.

15. Ibid., 1147a24–1147b19, as translated (and paraphrased) by David Wiggins in "Weakness of Will, Commensurability, and the Objects of Deliberation and Desire," in *Essays on Aristotle's Ethics,* 248–49.

16. Ibid., 1145b25.

17. Ibid., 1147a28.

18. Aristotle *De Anima* 434a5–10, as quoted in Wiggins, "Weakness of Will," 256.

19. Wiggins, "Weakness of Will," 256–57.

20. Davidson, *Essays on Actions and Events,* 41; "Reply to Essays I–X," 206.

21. Kant, *Groundwork,* 413 (37).

22. Beck, *A Commentary on Kant's Critique of Practical Reason,* 85; Kant, *Groundwork,* 417 (44–45).

23. Kant, *Groundwork,* 417–18 (45–46).

24. Cf. Alan Donagan, *The Theory of Morality,* 210–15.

25. Cf. Wiggins, "Weakness of Will," 254–62.

26. Cf. Bernard Williams, "Ought and Moral Obligation," 119.

27. Kant, *Groundwork,* 417 (45).

28. Ludwig Wittgenstein, *Philosophical Investigations,* trans. G. E. M. Anscombe, 3d ed. (New York: Macmillan, 1958), pt. 1, par. 217.

29. In the *Metaphysics of Morals,* pt. 2, p.385, Kant refers to "the rule of prudence in the choice of ends."

30. Davidson, *Essays on Actions and Events,* p. 41.

31. Aristotle *Nicomachean Ethics* 1146a27–30., 1151a30–35 (emphasis added).

32. Kant, *Critique of Pure Reason,* B ix, trans. Stephan Körner, in *Kant,* 129.

33. Kant defines an "interest" as the "dependence of a contingently determinable will on principles of reason" in the *Groundwork,* 413 n. (38 n.); cf. 460 n. (122 n.).

34. Lewis Carroll, *The Complete Works of Lewis Carroll* (London: Nonesuch Press, 1939), 1104–1108; Hare, "Rawls' Theory of Justice," 88; Anscombe, "Thought and Action in Aristotle," 69.

35. Wittgenstein, *Philosophical Investigations,* pt. 1, par. 210.

36. Cf. Anscombe, "Thought and Action in Aristotle," 69.

37. Kant, *Groundwork,* 431 (70–71).

38. Ibid., 460 n. (122 n.).

39. Ibid., 460–61 (122–23).

40. Ibid., 459 (121).

41. Wittgenstein, *Philosophical Investigations,* pt. 1, par. 217.

42. Ludwig Wittgenstein, *Tractatus Logico-Philosophicus*, trans. D. F. Pears and B. F. McGuinness (Routledge and Kegan Paul, 1922), 6.1–6.11; 6.113.

43. Ibid., 4.121.

44. Ludwig Wittgenstein, *On Certainty*, trans. Denis Paul and G. E. M. Anscombe (New York: Harper and Row, 1969), par. 204, cf. pars. 110, 559.

45. Ibid., pars. 501.

46. Hobbes, *Leviathan*, chap. 8, p. 139.

47. Kant, *Groundwork*, 437 (82).

48. Kant, *Critique of Practical Reason*, 43.

49. Kant, *Critique of Pure Reason*, A808, B836; *Religion within the Limits of Reason Alone*, 87–93, 139–41.

50. Cf. Paton, *The Categorical Imperative*, 140; Kant, *Groundwork*, 69.

51. Kant, *The Metaphysical Elements of Justice*, 231.

52. Beck, *A Commentary on Kant's Critique of Practical Reason*, 158–63.

53. Alasdair MacIntyre, *After Virtue*, 2d ed. (Notre Dame: University of Notre Dame Press, 1984), 46 (emphasis added).

54. The coherence of intentional action descriptions (satisfying 'p') implies that the intensional construal of actions must be qualified. As Davidson remarks, the description of the action "must also refer in rationalizations" (lest one say that 'S_1' acted intentionally, yet the action did not occur). *Essays on Actions and Events* (5). One observes the relevance of the Kantian dictum: "ought" implies "can" as the "reference" of action descriptions satisfying 'p' comprises the set of possible "objectively determined" (or determinable) events satisfying reason's pure, practical interest as expressed in prescriptive judgments of the form '$O(p)$.' My prescriptions would thus be practically exclusive for the domain of 'S,' i.e., if 'S_1' ought to perform 'A_1' under the description 'd_1' and if 'S_2' ought to perform 'A_2' under the description 'd_2', then it must be the case that 'A_1' and 'A_2' under the appropriate descriptions are existentially compossible (whether or not 'S_1' and 'S_2' are the same person). Cf. Bernard Williams, "Ought and Moral Obligation," 119.

55. Kant, *Groundwork*, 427–29 (64–68).

56. Dworkin, *Taking Rights Seriously*, 180–83, 272–78.

57. Kant, *Groundwork*, 436 n. (80 n.).

58. Kant, *Critique of Practical Reason*, 87.

59. Alan Gewirth, *Reason and Morality* (Chicago: University of Chicago Press, 1978), 171.

60. Ibid.

61. Ibid., 135, 176.

62. Kant, *Critique of Practical Reason*, 28.

63. Hare, "Do Agents Have to Be Moralists?" 56.

64. Kant, *Groundwork*, 434–35 (77).

65. Cf. Dworkin's observation that "we might . . . stipulate not to call any political aim a right unless it has a certain threshold weight against collective goals in general," in *Taking Rights Seriously*, 92.

66. Such an understanding corresponds to feminist philosophical criticism of the "generalized other." Cf. Seyla Benhabib, "The Generalized and

the Concrete Other," in *Situating the Self: Gender, Community, and Postmodernism in Contemporary Ethics* (New York: Routledge, 1992), 148–77; Iris Marion Young, "Impartiality and the Civic Public," in *Feminism as Critique*, ed. Seyla Benhabib and Drucilla Cornell (Minneapolis: University of Minnesota Press, 1987), 57–76.

67. Kant, *Groundwork*, 433–34 (74–75).

68. Kant, *Groundwork*, 433 (74). For an elaboration of the ethical implications of what I have described as the *telos* of normative consensus (albeit one resting upon a somewhat different interpretation of practical reason), cf. the assessment of Jürgen Habermas's theory of communicative action in chapter 6.

69. Cf. Henry Shue, *Basic Rights: Subsistence, Affluence, and U.S. Foreign Policy* (Princeton: Princeton University Press, 1980), 5–87.

70. Cf. Jürgen Habermas, "The Hermeneutic Claim to Universality," trans. Josef Bleicher, in Bleicher, *Contemporary Hermeneutics: Hermeneutics As Method, Philosophy, and Critique* (Boston: Routledge and Kegan Paul, 1980), 181–211.

6

On the Way to Hermeneutics

> *"All our dignity consists in thought. It is on that we must depend for our recovery. . . . Let us then strive to think well; that is the basic principle of morality."* [1]

PASCAL

In the preceding chapter, we interpreted prudential judgments as the expression of rational autonomy. Such judgments reflect reason's pure, practical interest (expressed as a conative propositional attitude in judgments of the form 'O(p)'): I prescribe that the intentions of practically rational agents 'S' be conformed to their best reasons, all things considered. My prudential prescriptions thus exhibit my pure, practical interest (formally generalized for 'S') in the formation of rationally coherent intentions.

As we argued in chapter 5, the condition of my subjection as 'S' to prudential prescription is my autonomy, for if I ought to perform an action under a certain description, then it must also be true *for me* that "I ought to perform the action." Reason's pure, practical interest, exhibited in my prescriptions, recurs, then, in a formal characterization of agents as rationally autonomous. In prescribing for myself *as* rationally autonomous, the pure, practical interest denominating me a rational (prudential) prescriber defines the intensional context within which *my* intentions are formed.

In the formation of my intentions, reason's interest is expressed in my disposition to regard my *best* reasons as decisive. A mere recitation of my "passions" as "original facts and realities, complete in themselves" would not, as Hume imagined, suffice to generate practical obligation; for I must form my best judgment, conditional upon all pertinent considerations.[2] Yet *my* best judgment, fittingly predicated of me as a rationally autonomous agent, is governed by my pure, practical interest, formally generalized for 'S', that 'S' act autonomously: my disposition, that is, to respect the rational autonomy of others as well as myself.

As we have seen in chapter 5, the formal object of reason's pure, practical interest is not this or that "producible" end but, rather, the reflective exhibition of 'S's rational autonomy in action, whence we may regard rationally autonomous agents as "ends in themselves." Prescribing for the domain of rationally autonomous agents 'S', I prescribe for a kingdom of ends that Kant describes as "a whole of ends in systematic conjunction (a whole both of rational beings as ends in themselves and also of the personal ends which each may set before himself.)."[3] For my prescriptions show forth my relation as a rationally autonomous prescriber to a possible kingdom of ends as the ideal, internal fruition of prudence.

Yet one might object that in skirting the Scylla of Kantian formalism, we have succumbed to the Charybdis of sophistic relativism. For in rendering the truth of objective, prudential judgments relative to the prescriber's "interest" in a kingdom of ends, we seem to fly in the face of the canons of empirical verification. Certainly, one could no longer abstract methodically from the beliefs and attitudes or "prejudices" of the one who judges. One wonders, then, if such judgments, rooted in custom and prejudice, merit the title of objectivity.

In response, I will argue in section (i) of the present chapter that prudential judgments are not uniquely susceptible to such criticism, for they form a subclass of phronetic judgments, falling under the general purview of philosophical hermeneutics. For Hans-Georg Gadamer, understanding in the human and social sciences (*Geisteswissenschaften*) can never be abstracted methodically from the situation of the interpreter. In section (ii), I will respond to the criticism that Gadamer's hermeneutical rehabilitation of "prejudice" fails to exorcise the specter of linguistic (and by implication, moral) relativism. For although Gadamer's own account of *phronēsis* remains somewhat ambivalent, I will argue that an analysis of "effective reflection," i.e., the reflective illumination of language in language, permits us to define the extension of "practical" truth for ordinary language. (In elucidating the role of prejudice in generating truth claims, I will appeal to Donald Davidson's account of the "application" of Tarski's "Convention 'T'" to natural languages.) Finally, in the third section, I will consider the moral implications of our critical reconstruction of *phronēsis* in light of Jürgen Habermas's critique of Gadamer's "neo-Aristotelian" hermeneutical program.

ON BEING AT HOME IN LANGUAGE

Heir to "the great tradition of practical (Aristotelian) philosophy," Gadamer's philosophical hermeneutics envisions the "virtue of practical rationality" (*phronēsis*) as a "model for the self-understanding of the human sciences."[4] For just as the knowledge of virtue, for the Aristotelian *phronimos*, implied his participation in the virtuous community, so for the human and social sciences our knowledge is always relative to the interpretative context of its application. The *subtilitas intelligendi* (understanding), the *subtilitas explicandi* (interpretation), and the *subtilitas applicandi* (application), which earlier hermeneutics distinguished, are for Gadamer inextricably linked as understanding understands itself.[5]

For Gadamer, our understanding is always, in the words of August Boeckh, a "knowing of the known."[6] For we are "always, already" at home in language, our world, already "organized in its basic relations into which experience steps as something new."[7] In our unfolding "stream of life and thought," in which, as Wittgenstein says, "our words have meaning," understanding is borne upon our linguistic traditions, revealing itself in our "flawed words and stubborn sounds."[8] Philosophy, for Gadamer, has no critical preamble from which, as Kant surmised, we might account for the transcendental conditions of the possibility of knowledge.[9] The ideal of a critical epistemology untrammeled by prejudice, indeed, reveals merely the Enlightenment's "prejudice against prejudice itself which denies tradition its power."[10]

Reflecting the rich heritage of our linguistic community, our prejudices do not merely limit but sustain understanding as the "biases of our openness to the world." Only the support of the "familiar and common understanding," the richly sedimented context of our preunderstandings or prejudice, permits "the broadening and enrichment of our own experience."[11] For our prejudices disclose the primordial "affinity of the one who understands to the one whom he understands and to that which he understands," so constituting "the initial schematization for all our possibilities of knowing."[12]

The "Hermeneutical Circle"

The affinity of knower and known, illumined in understanding, is explicated by Gadamer in terms of the metaphor of the "hermeneutical circle." For the "enrichment of our experience" presupposes our anticipatory apprehension of the subject matter—what Heidegger describes as our "fore-having, fore-sight, and fore-conceptions."[13] In textual interpretation, for instance, initial meanings emerge within an ever refined expectation of the meaning of the whole, so that "objectivity" (in interpretation) is the confirmation of our "fore-having, fore-sight, and fore-conception," culminating in the increment of knowledge.[14]

Our phronetic "knowing of the known" thus recalls Aristotle's resolution of the "sophistic puzzle" that virtue presumes *phronēsis* and *phronēsis*, virtue. For as moral goodness of character is the fruition of prudence, so the intentions of the *phronimos* are refined in the cultivation of virtue. The concrete instantiation (application) of the "right rule" of virtue enriches the "aesthetic" context of understanding, leading to ever finer discriminations of virtue. Yet the unveiling of the affinity of knower and known in our coming to understand is neither viciously circular nor merely to be tolerated. In its "positive ontological meaning," writes Gadamer, the hermeneutical circle describes not a methodological limitation of the human sciences but the "manner in which interpretation always proceeds when it intends an understanding tempered to the 'thing itself.'" For "in the circle is hidden," says Heidegger, "a positive possibility of the most primordial kind of knowing."[15]

The Fusion of Horizons

As intimated in our consideration of the hermeneutical circle, our understanding is "always, already" situated within the unfolding stream of life and thought. Our "knowing of the known" does not imply our attaining a transcendental perspective, independent of tradition; rather, our understanding is *an event of tradition, a process of transmission in which past and present are constantly mediated,*" a mediation that Gadamer describes as a "fusion of horizons."[16] The notion of horizon expresses the finite, temporal situation of our understanding as emerging from the constitutive matrix of pre-understanding or prejudice. For there is finally no "presuppositionless, 'prejudiceless'" understanding. As David Linge observes, while the interpreter "may free himself from this or that situation, he cannot free himself from his own facticity," i.e., from the "*ontological* condition of always already having a finite temporal situation as the horizon within which the beings he understands have their initial meaning for him."[17]

In seeking to understand a classical text such as the Scriptures, for instance, I cannot methodically prescind from my own "finite temporal situation" so as to reconstruct the mind of the author. "[T]he real meaning of a text, as it speaks to the interpreter, does not depend on the contingencies of the author and his original audience . . . for it is always co-determined also by the historical situation of the interpreter and hence by the totality of the objective course of history." Indeed, the "meaning of a text goes beyond its author" not "just occasionally but always."[18]

The meaning of Scripture is unfolded for me as, in the event of understanding, my perspective is reflectively mediated with that of the text. Understanding is described as a "fusion of horizons" inasmuch as my intentional "projections" or anticipations of meaning are "tempered" to the heritage of meaning constituted by the text. Our intentional horizons, while attesting our finite temporality, are, however, never closed; for in the "working of tradition," writes Gadamer, "this process of fusion is continually going on, for there old and new are always combining into something of living value, without either being explicitly foregrounded from the other."[19] One speaks not merely of "the pastness of the past," in Eliot's words, "but of its presence."[20]

The Hermeneutical Claim to Universality

Inspired by Heidegger's interpretation of Aristotelian *phronēsis* as "the way of disclosure," understanding, for Gadamer, is an unveiling within language of the affinity of the knower and the known.[21] The generation of truth claims thus implies the "priority of the 'relation' over against its relational members—the I who understands and that which is understood."[22] For Gadamer, understanding is not primarily a matter of the *adequatio intellectus et rei* but rather of the "disclosedness" of this affinity in the fusion of horizons.

The event of understanding reveals the "speculative" character of language, which for Gadamer signifies that "the finite possibilities of the word are oriented towards the sense intended as towards the infinite." One "speaks speculatively," writes Gadamer, when one's "words do not reflect beings, but express a *relation* to the *whole of being*," never itself expressly thematized.[23] Gadamer thus speaks of the "living virtuality" of discourse, as reflecting "the infinity of meaning to be explicated," the infinite "entirety of truth" that is shown forth in our saying.[24]

"It is this infinity of the unsaid—this relation to the whole of being that is disclosed in what *is* said—into which the one who understands is drawn."[25] So it is that we may conceive the hermeneutical claim to universality, for the act of saying is comprehended in its implicit, ontological orientation to "the whole of being." For Gadamer, indeed, understanding apprehends itself in the ever partial disclosedness (*alētheia*) of the infinite "wholeness of truth." The extension of truth claims is not limited by the finite particularity of language. For, writes Gadamer, the linguistic "form in which . . . understanding is interpreted must contain within it an infinite dimension that transcends all bounds." In the event of understanding, "the thinking reason escapes the prison of language, and is itself verbally [i.e., linguistically] constituted."[26]

But how, precisely, is one to "say" this, i.e., to speak, reflectively, of our knowledge of the known? For Gadamer, speculative reflection is never fulfilled in the "absolute knowledge" of Hegel. For the "truth of experience always implies an orientation toward new experience." The "dialectic of experience has its proper fulfillment not in definitive knowledge, but in the openness to experience that is made possible by experience itself."[27] A certain ambiguity characterizes the formulation, for Gadamer's assertions about the extension of truth might be regarded as self-limiting if truths concerning the "truth of experience" are themselves subject to mediation in "new experience." Were this so, one could no longer preclude the possibility of discrete, incommensurable language games. The perplexity, indeed, becomes paradoxical if the thesis of historicism (that all knowledge is historically conditioned) finally succumbs to the historical relativity of its own assertion, so that, as Gadamer says, "one day its thesis will no longer be considered true."[28]

One wonders if Gadamer, having denied the possibility of definitive knowledge, can consistently assert that our hermeneutical reflection confirms "Hegel's doctrine of the absolute spirit," i.e., that "with him we know about the manifoldness of the encounter with ourselves that reaches *beyond every historical conditionedness*."[29] Critics such as

Jürgen Habermas have objected that, in Gadamer's philosophical hermeneutics, "Hegel's experience of reflection shrinks to the awareness that we are delivered up" to an event in "which the conditions of rationality change irrationally according to time and place, epoch and culture."[30]

For Gadamer, conversely, Habermas's postulation of a "universal historical consciousness" that would lift "itself out of the multiple goals and conceptions of goal in social actions" is soon lost in "the ensuing twilight." The "goal of world history, the freedom of all" envisioned by Hegel, is "held in suspense," in "the remoteness of a 'bad infinity'" for which "the end keeps on delaying its arrival."[31] Yet how fragile an inheritance is Gadamer's own belief revealed to be— that the *telos* of freedom is "reason's highest principle," a principle that "never again can be shaken."[32] For this too would seem but one of the "multiple goals and conceptions of goal" lost in the ensuing twilight.

THE BOUNDS OF SENSE

The merits of such criticism, I believe, rest less in a recognition of prejudice's role than in Gadamer's failure to offer a sufficiently precise account of it. I will propose in these pages that a critical construal of the notion of "effective reflection," in which the self-illumination of language occurs, permits us to distinguish prejudices figuring in assertorial judgments (as the thematic objects of judgment) from those expressed in the reflective explication of "the truth of experience."

The "truth of experience" would, then, not be primarily that "of a single proposition . . . measured by its merely factual relationship of correctness and congruency," i.e., an "apophantic" judgment. Nor would "it depend merely upon the *context* in which it stands." For the "truth of experience" is not a truth "said" in a particular language game but, rather, what is "shown forth" in our saying—the reflective illumination of what it is for a judgment to be "true."[33]

In Wittgenstein's words, when "we first begin to *believe* anything, what we believe is not a single proposition, it is a whole system of propositions. (Light dawns gradually over the whole.)"[34] The metaphor is rich indeed, for we might speak of the "horizon" within which understanding illumines itself. In Gadamer's terms:

When our historical consciousness transposes itself into historical horizons, this does not entail passing into alien worlds unconnected in any way with our own; instead, they together constitute the one great horizon that moves from within and that, beyond the frontiers of the present, embraces the historical depths of our self-consciousness. Everything contained in historical consciousness is in fact embraced by a single historical horizon.[35]

A "linguistically constituted view of the world," as a system of beliefs, has not only its own truth *in itself*," writes Gadamer, "but also its own truth *for us*."[36] So construed, truth is not "relative" to a particular object domain, as defined by differing conceptual schemes or language games. It expresses rather the reflective illumination of language in language, as, in the multiplicity of our ways of saying, the "same unity of thought and speech" asserts itself.[37]

"Effective Reflection" (die "effektive" Reflexion)

For Gadamer, there is finally "no captivity within a language." For the coming to be of understanding in language is opened into the "infinite realm of possible expression," revealing the "infinity of the act" (of understanding) that "is linguistically creative and world experiencing."[38] In terms reminiscent of Heidegger's depiction of *Dasein* as the being in which the whole of being is illumined, Gadamer conceives our understanding as an unveiling within language of the infinite "entirety of truth."[39]

Our immersion in language does not imply "linguistic relativism," for in the unfolding dialectic of question and answer, understanding implies for Gadamer our "rising to a higher universality that overcomes not only our own particularity but also that of the other."[40] Our intentional horizons are porous, so that understanding (*Verständnis*), oriented in the fusion of horizons toward agreement (*Einverständnis*), is not fragmented into incommensurable language games.

Although our agreements may be surpassed or modified in the further "application" of understanding, understanding discloses itself in light of this "virtual" universality. The limits of each noetic accomplishment are transcended in the "inner infinity of discourse" opening "in the direction of the truth that we are."[41] The task of "understanding and interpreting" thus "always remains meaningful." For in its very concretion, understanding reveals the "superior universality with which reason rises above the limitations of any given language."[42]

Yet the inner illumination of understanding (our speaking of, and not merely, in language) cannot be attributed to a form of objectifying consciousness—what Gadamer describes, following Heidegger, as the *"actus signatus"* of objective signification. The virtuality of discourse is, rather, reflectively illumined in the *"actus exercitus"* of "effective reflection," i.e., the "inner reversal of intentionality in reflection, which in no way raises the thing meant to a thematic object." It is, indeed, only thus that the "enigmatic form of the being of language" may be grasped; for one must distinguish "effective reflection," in which "the unfolding of language takes place, from expressive and thematic reflection."[43]

As for Aristotle "every *aisthēsis* is an *aisthēsis aisthēseos*" (a perception of the perceiving), so each act of saying is reflectively illumined in its virtuality *as* discourse, i.e., as oriented toward the infinite wholeness of truth.[44] "The essence of language" would not, then, "consist entirely in being a means of giving information." For, as Heidegger recognized in his interpretation of Aristotelian *phronēsis*, the interior illumination of understanding describes a "mode of knowledge that could no longer be based in any way on a final objectifiability" of science.[45]

Reflectively illumined in discourse, the "truth of experience" reveals a common noetic horizon, tacitly assumed in the self-interpretation of language games. To the ever receding horizons, that, in Husserl's words, "open up to us, to our growing astonishment, an infinity of ever new phenomena," there corresponds our self-understanding as oriented in discourse to this infinity.[46] Our finite immersion in language, and the consequent denial of a moment of absolute knowledge, does not, then, imply a "bad infinity" of intermonadic or incommensurable language games. For our orientation to new experience is itself grasped within a common horizon, i.e., our anticipation of the "entirety of truth" disclosed in the fulfillment of intentionality.

We might thus conclude that every language game implies the universal horizon of its own comprehension. For language, writes Gadamer, is not a "delimited realm of the speakable over against which other realms that are unspeakable might stand. Rather language is all-encompassing." Indeed, there is finally nothing "fundamentally excluded from being said, to the extent that our act of meaning intends it. Our capacity for saying keeps pace untiringly with the universality of reason. Hence every dialogue also has an inner infinity and no end."[47]

"Convention 'T'"

As understanding apprehends itself in the fulfillment of intentionality—i.e., in the nonobjectifying *actus exercitus* of effective reflection—the universality proper to the *actus signatus* of understanding is disclosed. In analytical terms, effective reflection permits us to apprehend the scope of the signifying act (*actus signatus*), adumbrating a formal semantics.

Our analysis of hermeneutical self-reflection reveals certain affinities with Donald Davidson's admirably lucid account of a formal semantics for natural languages. For Davidson, as for Gadamer, our truth claims admit of interpretation inasmuch as a theory of truth must show what it is for a statement to be not merely "true for itself" but also "true for us." Indeed, Davidson's criticism of the scheme/content distinction in the philosophical theories of Kuhn, Feyerabend, and Putnam is intended to dispel the possibility of conceptual relativism resting upon a dualism of interpretative concepts and an "uninterpreted source of evidence."[48]

For Davidson, as for Gadamer, the possibility of translation into a familiar tongue is not merely stipulated, for the claim of mutual interpretability must be justified. One must thus entertain the empiricist assumption that translation might be a problem (as, for instance, for Quine "the test of difference remains failure or difficulty of translation").[49] Upon empiricist assumptions, language is regarded as an empirical artifact (a mere tool) that may vary in composition over time, giving rise to successive theories that, writes Kuhn, "are thus, we say, incommensurable."[50]

Conceptual schemes so construed, writes Davidson, "either *organize* something, or they *fit* it" (as in Quine's remark that one "warps his scientific heritage to fit his . . . sensory promptings").[51] In the former case, it is not entirely clear what "organizing" a world signifies, since presumably the notion of a world as uniformly delineated or differentiable into elements that might be organized is already a matter of interpretation. Yet once we concede that there are various "objects" to be organized antecedently bearing the mark of interpretation, we are in Strawson's (or Gadamer's), rather than Kuhn's, universe.

Davidson argues that differences in the extension of predicates presume for their very intelligibility a common ontology of language in which concepts "individuate the same objects."[52] Predicative distinction, that is, presupposes a semantical continuity, which, it would seem, is consistent with Wittgenstein's observation that "[i]f someone says, 'If our language had not this grammar, it could not express these facts'—it should be asked what 'could' means here."[53] In the words of Gadamer, our world is always, already interpreted, already "organized in its basic relations, into which experience steps as something new."

For an empiricist theory, writes Davidson, fitting the "totality of possible sensory evidence" would imply its truth. What a theory says about physical objects, number, or sets would be true if the theory "as a whole fits the sensory evidence." So construed, such "entities might be called posits."[54] The assumption is that sensory experience is distinguished from what is posited; the distinction, however, is itself "posited" in such fashion that sensory experience must serve as its own criterion of admissibility as evidence, inviting an infinite regression.

The gravamen of Davidson's criticism is that such a dualism of concept (or language) and uninterpreted object is finally inconsistent with what it means for a claim to be "true for us," as epitomized in the application of Tarski's "Convention 'T'" to natural languages. For the notions of "fitting the totality of experience," or "fitting the facts," or "being true to the facts," writes Davidson, add "nothing intelligible" to the simple notion of "being true."[55] With the qualification of indexical features proper to natural languages, the notion "being true" is formalized in Tarski's "Convention 'T'." "While the words 'designates,' 'satisfies,' and 'defines' express relations . . . , the word 'true' is of a different logical nature: it expresses a property (or denotes a class) of certain expressions, viz., of sentences."[56]

All theories of truth for a language 'L' must accordingly entail, writes Davidson, "for every sentence 's' of 'L', a theorem of the form 's' is true if and only if 'p' where 's' is replaced by a description of 's' and 'p' by 's' itself if 'L' is English, and by a translation of 's' into English if 'L' is not English." Since the true sentences of any conceptual scheme must be, ex hypothesi, "true" in this sense (and if one admits a certain internal differing on details), it follows that the criterion of a conceptual scheme differing from our own "now becomes: largely true but not translatable."[57]

Although sentences like "'Snow is white' is true if and only if snow is white" are in one sense trivially true, conveying no novel information, they do, nonetheless, exhibit a characteristic "property" of language. For the totality of such sentences would uniquely determine the extension of the concept of truth for 'L', in this case English. Yet this implies, as we have seen, that for any sentence 's' of 'L' that is not English, "'s' is true if and only if 'p'," where 's' is replaced by a description of 's' and 'p' by a translation (or interpretation) of 's' into English. As a property of sentences, "being true" is thus relative to the perspective of the interpreter. In Gadamer's words, each linguistic worldview (or conceptual scheme) "potentially contains every other one within it—i.e., each worldview can be extended into every other. It can understand and comprehend, from within itself, the 'view' of the world presented in another language," with the consequence that truth is exhibited in the intertranslatability of sentences.[58]

Imagining a language in which this failed to obtain, conversely, is to not imagine a language. One thinks, in this respect, of Wittgenstein's remark that the "common behaviour of mankind is the system of reference by means of which we interpret an unknown language."[59] For, reflectively explicated, the system of reference to which Wittgenstein alludes might be taken to include Convention 'T' as embodying, in Davidson's words, "our best intuition as to how the concept of truth is used."[60]

Our common linguistic behavior, illumined reflectively, thus attests "the universality of reason," which for Gadamer determined the virtuality of discourse. The hermeneutical claim to universality in the mutual interpretability of language games is not true by mere fiat of stipulation. Its warrants, rather, become apparent as we reflect upon what a theory of truth for any language 'L' must entail.

What is the logical force of this "must"? It is, as we have suggested, not arbitrarily assumed, for we are not at liberty to define 'L' otherwise and hence cannot imagine 'L_1' in which Convention 'T' failed to obtain. Similarly, Convention 'T', as logically prior to a semantical "definition" of truth, is not empirically defeasible; one cannot chance upon 'L_1'. That Convention 'T' is exhibited for all 'L' is a properly philosophic utterance, reflecting what is shown but not said.

Convention 'T' may thus be conceived as one of the limits of our language, and hence one of the limits of "our world." As disclosed in effective reflection (a distinctive Gadamerian contribution, largely wanting in Wittgenstein's analysis of language games), it is not a limit *in* our world, not an empirical artifact that could conceivably have been otherwise. As the semantical continuity of conceptual individuation must be assumed for any 'L', so must one assume the mutual interpretability presumed by our "common behaviour." For our "saying" shows forth the uniquely necessary conditions of its possibility.

Our brief excursus into Davidson's formal semantics reveals the internal correlation of understanding, interpretation, and application (of Convention 'T') as revealed in our common linguistic behavior. The "virtuality of discourse" as oriented toward the "wholeness of truth" would not define a distinctive metalanguage but is, rather, disclosed in the self-illumination of any language (rich enough to contain its own truth predicate).[61]

As the formal rules of logic, Convention 'T' may be construed analytically as a tautology, but as we have seen, such "prejudices" are far from trivial, for they are always, already "performatively at play" in the reflective illumination of language.[62] As the "scaffolding of our thoughts," they permit us to understand our "common behaviour," so as to "envisage in a fundamentally universal way what *always* happens."[63]

ETHICS AND HERMENEUTICS

Our hermeneutical appropriation of *phronēsis* suggests that a theory of practical truth need not entail a methodical abstraction from prejudice. For our entitlement to "objective" prescription would be sustained if prudential judgments could be shown to be *true for us* such that Convention 'T' is applicable in the practical realm. It must be the case, that is, that "'S' ought to perform 'A' under a certain description" is true if, and only if, 'S' ought to perform 'A' under the said description.

As effective reflection illumined the affinity of knower and known, so reflection in the practical realm disclosed the affinity of the one who prescribes to a possible kingdom of ends. Conative judgments of the form 'O(p)' show forth my pure, practical interest in realizing such a realm, so that for all rationally autonomous agents, the mutual interpretability of truth claims in the practical realm is assumed in accordance with Convention 'T'. For the domain of rationally autonomous agents, if 'A' is fittingly described as that which 'S_1' has best reason(s) to do, then 'S_1' ought to perform 'A' so described.

As my pure, practical interest is "shown forth" in my practical (prudential) prescriptions, i.e., in the *actus exercitus* of prescribing, it is not to be counted among the merely subjective, "producible" ends that numerically distinguish agents. For my anticipatory apprehension of a kingdom of ends (denominating me a rational prescriber) contributes to my initial characterization as a rationally *autonomous* agent. The formation of *my* intentions occurs within the intensional context defined by my pure, practical interest, so that the interpretation of my reasons reflects my respect for the rationally coherent intentions of others as "the supreme limiting condition of all subjective ends."[64]

Our intentions are tempered by the regulative ideal of a kingdom of ends, as the "personal ends each [agent] may set before himself" are brought "into conformity with this Idea." Our "mutual interest" in "a whole of ends in systematic conjunction" is fulfilled in a fusion of our intentional horizons, in our attaining and sustaining a rational consensus about "what can be made actual by our conduct," i.e., the *universale concretum* of a kingdom of ends.[65] Disclosed in "effective reflection," our anticipatory apprehension of a kingdom of ends is thus not a "prejudice" to be surmounted in practical judgment but, rather, the very condition of the possibility of our attaining "practical truth," i.e., "truth in accordance with right appetition" as our "self-knowledge" as citizens of a kingdom of ends is exhibited in autonomous action.

The Hermeneutical Critique of Jürgen Habermas

The import of our critical reconstruction of *phronēsis* is perhaps best illuminated against the background of Habermas's criticism. As we have seen, for Habermas, Gadamer's hermeneutical rehabilitation of "prejudice" finally succumbs to the "undialectical" positing of the "facticity of tradition."[66] In the earlier stages of his criticism, Habermas argued from the perspective of a critical epistemology for the necessity of a "controlled distanciation" (*Verfremdung*) from the "irrationalism" of traditions, which alone could "raise understanding from a prescientific experience" to the status "of a reflected procedure."[67] Only a "quasi-transcendental" moral critique of discursive traditions would suffice to redress the "systematic distortions" latent in communicative interaction.[68] One must, says Habermas, go "beyond hermeneutic consciousness" so as to "clarify the conditions for the possibility to, as it were, step outside the dialogical structure of everyday language and to use language in a monological way for the formal construction of theories and for the organization of purposive rational action."[69]

In his later writings, Habermas rejects the "*via regia*" of an epistemological critique, accepting, with Gadamer, the discursive redemption of (objective) practical validity claims.[70] Yet the primacy of a self-reflective, emancipatory critique of the "ethical substance" of traditions persists. While Gadamer upholds the primacy of *phronēsis* for practical discourse, Habermas distinguishes three "employments of practical reason" in terms reminiscent of Kant: the "pragmatic," the "ethical," and "the moral." The pragmatic or "purposive" employment of practical reason is expressed in the "semantic form of conditional imperatives" devoted to discovering the "appropriate techniques, strategies, or programs."[71] Where, however, our ends, or in Charles Taylor's terms, our "strong preferences," are themselves at issue, we appeal to practical reason (*phronēsis*) to elucidate our understanding of "the good life."[72]

Moral discourse, conversely, emerges amidst the ethical (*sittlich*) pluralism of modernity: "ethical questions point in a different direction from moral questions," which determine "the regulation of interpersonal conflicts of action resulting from opposed interests."[73] Gadamer's "neo-Aristotelian" hermeneutics, argues Habermas, fails to sustain the universal purview proper to moral discourse (i.e., Kant's formal elaboration of the categorical imperative). In a Kantian vein, Habermas "sharply" distinguishes our differing, prudential interpretations of *eudaimonia* from the formal, impartial requirements of morality (*Moralität*). Yet Habermas acknowledges the lacunae of Kant's critique, e.g., the insufficiency of moral prescription to which we have alluded in chapter 2. Formal, deontological constraints are not generated "independently of experience" but, rather, imposed upon ethical (prudential) judgment, such that the *intersubjective* redemption of practical validity claims is assumed ab ovo: one no longer legislates from the monological perspective of *homo noumenon*.[74] Only a de facto consensus, attained in argument approximating the conditions of an ideal "unlimited communication community (unlimited, that is, in social space and historical time)" will suffice for the generation of valid (objective) claims.[75]

Unlike the pragmatic or ethical realms, which accept our ends or strong preferences *de trop*, the moral domain is concerned with rational (autonomous) will-formation.[76] For it is in virtue not of a material specification of our ends that morality legislates but, rather, of the formal, procedural principle prescribing that a moral norm is valid if, and only if, "*[a]ll* affected can accept the consequences and the side effects its *general* observance can be anticipated to have for the satisfaction of *everyone's* interests (and these consequences are preferred to those of known alternative possibilities for regulation)."[77] Habermas's principle of universalization ("U") rests upon a "transcendental-pragmatic" justification inasmuch as every agent tacitly acknowledges it on pain of performative or pragmatic contradiction.[78]

From the ethical (hermeneutical) perspective of the *phronimos*, the requirements of universalization represent a merely "regulative" or extrinsic constraint *imposed* upon prudential deliberation, which of itself remains ethnocentric, if not egoistic.[79] Yet one wonders if Habermas's formal, procedural interpretation of the categorical imperative does not finally fall prey to the very *aporiae* besetting the theories of Kant and his heirs. For, as we saw in chapters 2, 3, and 4, the *separation* of the moral and ethical domains, of *Moralität* and *Sittlichkeit*, gave credence to Hegel's criticism of "empty formalism." Indeed, it was only by recurring to our moral *experience* and, in particular, to our phronetic self-knowledge as members of a moral commonwealth that our practical claims were redeemed.

As we argued in chapter 2, Rawls surmounts the limits of Kant's first, formal formulation of the supreme moral law by implicitly invoking the second (i.e., the "material" principle of respect for persons); yet, as Habermas quite rightly observes, with "the shifting of normative premises from the procedure to the concept of the person already undertaken in the Dewey Lectures, Rawls presents an unprotected flank to the familiar neo-Aristotelian objections."[80] Now it is precisely these "familiar neo-Aristotelian objections" (i.e., Rawls's dependence upon "a substantive normative concept of the person") that Habermas himself must finally acknowledge.[81] For Habermas's interpretation of "U" presupposes not only that affected agents accept the consequences and the side effects that the *general* observance of a maxim can be anticipated to have for the satisfaction of *everyone's* interests but also that their acceptance is consistent with what Rawls terms agents' "moral powers" and their correlative "*highest-order interests*" in their exercise, i.e., respect for persons as comprising a kingdom of ends.

Merely formal, procedural stipulations of impartiality will not suffice, for, as Bernard Williams observes, "under conditions of exploitation" agents' consciousness of their own activities "may be suppressed or destroyed." The more extreme the degradation, indeed, the more likely it is that its victims "do *not* see themselves differently from the way they are seen by the exploiters; either they do not see themselves as anything at all, or they acquiesce passively in the role for which they have been cast."[82] Criticism of such "systematic distortions" presumes, in Habermas's own words, "the symmetrical respect that everyone should accord the integrity of all other persons."[83]

As we argued in the preceding chapter, attaining and sustaining an "ideal" consensus rests finally upon "the communicative *presuppositions* of an inclusive and noncoercive discourse among free and equal partners."[84] Just as for Rawls, impartial consensus finally presumes a "normative concept of the person," i.e., Habermas's tacit "prejudice" of "equal respect for all." The effective "telos" of attaining an ideal consensus, i.e., one "without repression," thus implies that not all "interests" or "prejudices" are on the same moral footing.[85] For, as we argued in our hermeneutical reconstruction of *phronēsis*, deliberation with a view to attaining consensus presumes the antecedent recognition (*sunesis*) of mutual respect of agents already citizens of a kingdom of ends.

While the latter, ethical ideal may be interpreted and applied in as yet unforeseen circumstances, it cannot, from our hermeneutical perspective, be radically problematized.[86] For the "rights" of certain prejudices must be respected: the maxim of respect functions *constitutively* in determining our self-knowledge (and not merely regulatively) in the generation of valid moral claims, so that raising *it* into question is to outstrip the bounds of sense.[87] The ideal of respect, as the *intrinsic* finality or *telos* of ethical (hermeneutical) discourse, limns the boundaries of what Rawls calls our *reasonable*, comprehensive understandings of the good.[88] We need not, in Habermas's words, "step outside" the hermeneutical circle, for it is already bounded by a kingdom of ends.

Our phronetic interpretation of Kant's kingdom is, of course, no mere repristination of Aristotle's *polis*. For the burden of our argument has been not so much the retrieval of Aristotelian ethics (e.g., Alasdair MacIntyre's neo-Aristotelian ethics) as a defense of the unity of practical reason, i.e., of *Moralität* and *Sittlichkeit*. The semantic constraints upon a reasonable theory of the good imposed by *phronēsis* are not simply "formal and empty," in Habermas's words, but entail the material recognition of respect for persons, so that we may speak of a common finality, or *telos*, a common good irreducible to a mere congeries of individual interests.[89]

As we have conceived it, *phronēsis* is not merely devoted to the replication of particular forms of life, each with its discrete conceptualization of the good; instead, *phronēsis* legislates for the personal and institutional embodiment of the maxim of respect. Pace Habermas, rational will-formation unfolds under the aspect of the good, albeit a *common* good, interpreted and applied (as the virtue of "solidarity") in varied historical and cultural settings.[90] Its universality is perforce "concrete," yet sufficiently determinate to decry the *moral* tragedy of any child who goes to bed hungry, any tortured dissident, any woman suffering discrimination. The "moral teleology" explicated in the previous chapter thus comes to fruition not merely in the "rights of prejudice" but in the "prejudice of rights." For inasmuch as the maxim of respect implies the conditions of its application, we may say that the basic, structural ideal of the common good is specified by a regime of basic rights—in the words of Ignacio Ellacuría, the "union of structural conditions" presumed (even by Habermas) for fair and impartial choice.[91]

CONCLUDING REFLECTIONS

In these pages, I have defended a conception of the unity of practical reason that charts a via media between the abstract formalism of Kantian *Moralität* in its differing formulations, and Hegelian *Sittlichkeit*, no longer unified in the sublation of "Objective Spirit." With Gadamer, we argued on behalf of the cognitive role of prejudices in the redemption of valid moral claims but, with Habermas, noted the ambivalence of Gadamer's invocation of *phronēsis* in the ethical domain. Our appeal to the constitutive role of the "prejudice" of respect for persons in prudential (phronetic) judgments, moreover, permitted us to redress the lacunae of Habermas's justification of "U" without thereby divesting our moral norms of formal, pragmatic justification.

Our reflections have not aspired to offer an algorithmic procedure for responding to the Socratic question "How should one live?" For our conception of respect is not a supreme deductive principle of theoretical inquiry, logically independent of the context of its application. Like an obbligato occurring in countless variations, the principle of respect may be elaborated in differing (non-uniform) maxims. Its universality must be concretely expressed in our attaining and sustaining rational consensus in the *aisthēsis* of rationally autonomous behavior. Ideals admit of revision, even as the natural law was "changeable" for Aristotle.[92] Yet reason, though parsimonious, is not wholly quiescent. Even for Beckett, there are leaves on the tree.

NOTES TO CHAPTER 6

1. Blaise Pascal, *Pensées*, trans. A. J. Krailsheimer (Harmondsworth, England: Penguin Books, 1966), (347), 95.
2. Hume, *A Treatise of Human Nature*, (490), 9.
3. Kant, *Groundwork*, 433 (74).
4. Hans-Georg Gadamer, "Hermeneutics as Practical Philosophy," in *Reason in the Age of Science*, trans. Frederick G. Lawrence (Cambridge: MIT Press, 1981), 111; "The Problem of Historical Consciousness," trans. Jeff L. Close, in *Interpretative Social Science: A Reader*, ed. Paul Rabinow and William M. Sullivan (Berkeley: University of California Press, 1979), 107.
5. Gadamer, *Truth and Method*, 307–308, 398.
6. Cf. August Boeckh, *Encyklopädie und Methodologie der philologische Wissenschaften*, ed. Ernst Bratuscheck (Leipzig: Teubner, 1877), as quoted in Gadamer, "On the Problem of Self-Understanding," in *Philosophical Hermeneutics*, trans. and ed. David E. Linge (Berkeley: University of California Press, 1976), 45.
7. Gadamer, "The Universality of the Hermeneutical Problem," in *Philosophical Hermeneutics*, 15.
8. Ludwig Wittgenstein, *Zettel*, trans. G. E. M. Anscombe (Oxford: Basil Blackwell, 1967), par. 173; Stevens, "The Poems of Our Climate," 158.
9. In the section of *Truth and Method* entitled "Language As Horizon of a Hermeneutic Ontology," Gadamer asserts that

> the infinite perfectibility of the human experience of the world means that, whatever language we use, we never succeed in seeing anything but an ever more extended aspect, a "view" of the world. Those views of the world are not relative in the sense that one could oppose them to the "world in itself," as if the right view from some possible position outside the human, linguistic world could discover it in its being-in-itself (447).

10. Gadamer, *Truth and Method*, 270.
11. Gadamer, "The Universality of the Hermeneutical Problem," 9, 15.
12. Gadamer, "The Heritage of Hegel," in *Reason in the Age of Science*, 48; "The Universality of the Hermeneutical Problem," 13.

13. Martin Heidegger, *Being and Time*, trans. John Macquarrie and Edward Robinson (New York: Harper and Row, 1962), 195; as quoted in Gadamer, "The Problem of Historical Consciousness," 148; cf. *Truth and Method*, 265–71.

14. Gadamer, *Truth and Method*, 267, 269.

15. Gadamer, "The Problem of Historical Consciousness," 148–49; Heidegger; *Being and Time*, 195.

16. Gadamer, *Truth and Method*, 290; cf. 306–307, 374–75, 388, 397, 576.

17. David E. Linge, editor's introduction to Gadamer's *Philosophical Hermeneutics*, xlvii; cf. Gadamer, *Truth and Method*, 293.

18. Gadamer, *Truth and Method*, 296.

19. Ibid., 306.

20. T. S. Eliot, "Tradition and the Individual Talent," in *Criticism: The Major Texts*, ed. Walter Jackson Bate (New York: Harcourt, Brace and World, 1952), 525.

21. Cf. Gadamer, "The Heritage of Hegel," 48.

22. Gadamer, "On the Problem of Self-Understanding," in *Philosophical Hermeneutics*, 50.

23. Gadamer, *Truth and Method*, 469 (emphasis added).

24. Gadamer, *Truth and Method*, 458; *Hegel's Dialectic: Five Hermeneutical Studies*, trans. P. Christopher Smith (New Haven: Yale University Press, 1976), 96–97. Cf. Francis J. Ambrosio, "Gadamer: On Making Oneself at Home with Hegel," *The Owl of Minerva* 19, no. 1 (1987): 23–40.

25. Linge, editor's introduction to Gadamer's *Philosophical Hermeneutics*, xxxii.

26. Gadamer, *Truth and Method*, 401–402.

27. Gadamer, *Truth and Method*, 355.

28. Ibid., 534.

29. Gadamer, "The Heritage of Hegel," 53 (emphasis added).

30. Jürgen Habermas, "A Review of Gadamer's *Truth and Method*," in *Understanding and Social Inquiry*, ed. Fred R. Dallmayr and Thomas A. McCarthy (Notre Dame: University of Notre Dame Press, 1977), 359; cf. also 354. Cf. Paul Ricoeur, "Hermeneutics and the Critique of Ideology," in *Hermeneutics and the Human Sciences: Essays on Language, Action and Interpretation*, ed. and trans. John B. Thompson (Cambridge: Cambridge University Press, 1981), 75. "Gadamer's account," writes Ricoeur, "is similar to Hegel's, insofar as historical comprehension requires a 'common understanding concerning the thing' and hence a unique *logos* of communication; but Gadamer's position is only tangential to that of Hegel, because his Heideggerian ontology of finitude prevents him from transforming this unique horizon into a knowledge."

31. Gadamer, "On the Scope and Function of Hermeneutical Reflection," in *Philosophical Hermeneutics*, 28; "The Heritage of Hegel," 40, 59–60.

32. Gadamer, "Hegel's Philosophy and Its Aftereffects until Today," in *Reason in the Age of Science*, 37.

33. Gadamer, "The Heritage of Hegel," 44 (emphasis added).

34. Wittgenstein, *On Certainty*, par. 141 (emphasis added).

35. Gadamer, *Truth and Method*, 304.

36. Ibid., 442, 447.

37. Ibid., 402.

38. Gadamer, "The Universality of the Hermeneutical Problem," 15–16.

39. Cf. Martin Heidegger, "Letter on Humanism," trans. Frank A. Capuzzi and J. Glenn Gray, in *Martin Heidegger: Basic Writings*, ed. David Farrell Krell (New York: Harper and Row, 1977), 213–23.

40. Gadamer, "The Universality of the Hermeneutical Problem," 15–16; *Truth and Method*, 305.

41. Gadamer, "The Universality of the Hermeneutical Problem," 16.

42. Gadamer, *Truth and Method*, 402.

43. Gadamer, "On the Scope and Function of Hermeneutical Reflection," 35.

44. Gadamer, "The Philosophical Foundations of the Twentieth Century," in *Philosophical Hermeneutics*, 123.

45. Martin Heidegger, "Hölderlin and the Essence of Poetry," trans. Douglas Scott, in *Existence and Being*, ed. Werner Brock (Chicago: Henry Regnery, 1949), 276; Gadamer, "Heidegger and Marburg Theology," in *Philosophical Hermeneutics*, 201–202.

46. Edmund Husserl, *The Crisis of European Sciences and Transcendental Phenomenology*, trans. David Carr (Evanston, Ill.: Northwestern University Press, 1970), 112.

47. Gadamer, "Man and Language," in *Philosophical Hermeneutics*, 67.

48. Donald Davidson, *Inquiries into Truth and Interpretation* (Oxford: Clarendon Press, 1984), xviii. Such a dualism of concept (or language) and object, as Davidson observes, differs from Strawson's distinction of concept and content, in terms of which various logically possible worlds might be imaginatively construed from within the semantical horizon of our own.

49. W. V. Quine, "Speaking of Objects," in *Ontological Relativity and Other Essays* (New York: Columbia University Press, 1969), 25.

50. T. S. Kuhn, "Reflections on My Critics," in *Criticism and the Growth of Knowledge*, ed. I. Lakatos and A. Musgrave (Cambridge: Cambridge University Press, 1970), 266–67.

51. Davidson, "On the Very Idea of a Conceptual Scheme," in *Inquiries into Truth and Interpretation*, 191; W. V. Quine, "Two Dogmas of Empiricism," in *From a Logical Point of View*, 2d ed. (Cambridge: Harvard University Press, 1961), 46.

52. Davidson, "On the Very Idea of a Conceptual Scheme," 192.

53. Wittgenstein, *Philosophical Investigations*, pt. 1, par. 497.

54. Davidson, "On the Very Idea of a Conceptual Scheme," 193.

55. Ibid., 194.

56. A. Tarski, "The Semantic Conception of Truth," *Philosophy and Phenomenological Research* 4 (1944), 345. Cf. Donald Davidson, "In Defence of Convention T," in *Inquiries into Truth and Interpretation*, 64–75.

57. Davidson, "On the Very Idea of a Conceptual Scheme," 194.

58. Gadamer, *Truth and Method*, 448.

59. Wittgenstein, *Philosophical Investigations*, pt. 1, par. 206.

60. Davidson, "On the Very Idea of a Conceptual Scheme," 195.

61. In formally regimented discourse, the language in which reflection occurs would represent the semantically richer language in which truth is predicated of the object language.

62. Gadamer, "Hermeneutics as Practical Philosophy," in *Reason in the Age of Science*, 112.

63. Gadamer, *Truth and Method*, 512.

64. Kant, *Groundwork*, 431 (70).

65. Ibid., 433 (74), 436 n. (80 n.)

66. Habermas, "A Review of Gadamer's *Truth and Method*," 358.

67. Ibid., 355, 359.

68. Habermas, "The Hermeneutic Claim to Universality," 189.

69. Ibid., 188.

70. Jürgen Habermas, "A Philosophico-Political Profile," in *Habermas: Autonomy and Solidarity*, ed. and trans. Peter Dews (London: New Left Books, 1986), 152–53; cf. *The Theory of Communicative Action*, vol. 1, 273–337.

71. Jürgen Habermas, *Justification and Application: Remarks on Discourse Ethics*, trans. Ciaran P. Cronin (Cambridge: MIT Press, 1993), 3.

72. Ibid., 4; cf. Charles Taylor, "The Concept of a Person," in *Philosophical Papers* (Cambridge: Cambridge University Press, 1985), 1:97–114; and *Sources of the Self: The Making of the Modern Identity* (Cambridge: Harvard University Press, 1989), 14–19, 42.

73. Habermas, *Justification and Application*, 6.

74. Ibid., 1–2. Cf. Jürgen Habermas, *The Philosophical Discourse of Modernity*, trans. Frederick Lawrence (Cambridge: MIT Press, 1987), 294–335.

75. Cf. Habermas, *Justification and Application*, 163. For Habermas's earlier appeal to an "ideal speech situation," cf. "Toward a Theory of Communicative Competence," *Inquiry* 13 (1970): 372.

76. Habermas, *Justification and Application*, 8–10, 14–17.

77. Jürgen Habermas, *Moral Consciousness and Communicative Action*, trans. Christian Lenhardt and Shierry Weber Nicholsen (Cambridge: MIT Press, 1990), 65.

78. Ibid., 76–109.

79. Cf. Habermas's observation that "[e]thical questions by no means call for a complete break with the egocentric perspective; in each instance they take their orientation from the telos of one's own life." *Justification and Application*, 6.

80. Habermas, *Justification and Application*, 178 n. 12.

81. Ibid., 28.

82. Bernard Williams, "The Idea of Equality," 237.

83. Habermas, *Justification and Application*, 6.

84. Ibid., 52 (emphasis added).

85. Ibid., 6, 13, 53. Cf. Habermas, "The Hermeneutic Claim to Universality," 205.

86. Cf., in contrast, Habermas's assertion that "[w]ithin the horizon of the lifeworld, practical judgments derive both their concreteness and their power to motivate action from their inner connection to unquestioningly accepted ideas of the good life, in short, from their connection to ethical life and its institutions. Under these conditions, problematization can never be so profound as to risk all the assets of the existing ethical substance. But the abstractive achievements required by the moral point of view do precisely that." *Moral Consciousness and Communicative Action*, 108–109.

87. Habermas, "A Review of Gadamer's *Truth and Method*, 358. Cf. Habermas's assessment of regulative and constitutive ideas in *Justification and Application*, 164–65. While the "schema of world-constitution is inapplicable" in the practical realm, the regulative ideal of an "unlimited communication community," adumbrated in our own argument in terms of Kant's "kingdom of ends," must be presupposed *"as a matter of fact,"* even if its ideal content can only be approximated in reality. Yet while Habermas argues that "the regulative idea of the validity of utterances is constitutive for the social facts produced through communicative action," we have attended, rather, to the *self-knowledge* of the agents themselves (i.e., as constituting such a kingdom).

88. Rawls, *Political Liberalism*, 48–66.

89. Habermas, *Justification and Application*, 47.

90. Habermas himself intimated as much when he wrote in the appendix to *Knowledge and Human Interests*, trans. Jeremy J. Shapiro (Boston: Beacon Press, 1971) 314, that:

> only in an emancipated society, whose members' autonomy and responsibility had been realized, would communication have developed into the non-authoritarian and universally practiced dialogue from which both our model of reciprocally constituted ego identity and our idea of true consensus are always implicitly derived. To this extent the truth of statements is based on *anticipating the realization of the good life* [emphasis added].

91. Ignacio Ellacuría, "Human Rights in a Divided Society," in *Human Rights in the Americas: The Struggle for Consensus* ed. Alfred Hennelly and John Langan (Washington, D.C.: Georgetown University Press, 1982), 56. Such a construal, I believe, illumines the logical correlation of dignity, human rights, and the common good in modern Roman Catholic social teaching. Cf. David Hollenbach, "The Common Good Revisited," *Theological Studies* 50 (1989): 70–94; John Coleman, "Catholic Human Rights Theory: Four Challenges to an Intellectual Tradition," *Journal of Law and Religion* 2 (1984): 343–66.

92. See Gadamer, *Truth and Method*, 319.

7

A Concluding Theological Postscript

"In a flash, at a trumpet crash,
I am all at once what Christ is, since he was what I am, and
This Jack, joke, poor potsherd, patch, matchwood, immortal
diamond,
Is immortal diamond."[1]

GERARD MANLEY HOPKINS

Disenchantment with the abstract formalism of Kantian *Moralität* inspires not only neo-Aristotelian ethics but distinctively religious ethical interpretations. Stanley Hauerwas espouses a "narrative ethics" in "a fragmented world of many moralities,"[2] while Karl Barth defends "the theonomy of human existence and action."[3] And yet other theologians, in a Kantian vein, regard Jesus's teaching as merely hortatory, bidding us abide by "a universal human morality."[4] "The requirements of morality as Jesus preached them," says Bruno Schüller, "are inherently accessible to natural reason."[5] Our quest for a via media between Kantian formalism and ethical relativism thus appears in a religious guise as we ask whether, or in what respects, ethics is "distinctively Christian."[6]

"What is the answer?" compels us to ask, like Gertrude Stein on her deathbed, "What is the question?" For theologians differ not merely as to whether but as to how Christian morality might be "distinctive." If for Karl Barth the "theonomy of human existence" implies that there is "no good which is not obedience to God's Command," for Josef Fuchs a "true *theonomous* ethics" has its foundation in the precepts of "the natural law."[7] The answers thus recur as questions at a higher level as one seeks to determine whether a "*true* theonomous ethics" is distinctively Christian. In this chapter, I will consider (i) the criticisms of moral theory raised in the theological ethics of Barth and Hans Urs von Balthasar, and the response of the "autonomy school" of Fuchs and Bruno Schüller. Our hermeneutical reconciliation of the rival schools (ii) brings our reflections to a suitably irenic conclusion.

THEOLOGICAL INTERPRETATIONS

Theological ethics is often bedeviled by a failure to distinguish the differing senses of how morality might be distinctively Christian—how, that is, the predicate "Christian" qualifies (i) the justification of moral rules or norms and (ii) the morally relevant description of action. A moral rule prescribing that "'S' ought to do 'A'," e.g., keep her promises, would be distinctively Christian, we might say, if its *justification* exhibits logical dependence upon Christian faith, i.e., the reasons vindicating or verifying it refer to distinctive Christian attitudes and beliefs, or if its justification is epistemically restricted to the domain of Christians, i.e., only (or primarily) Christians are in possession of the relevant moral knowledge. Were the precept of promise keeping to derive its prescriptive force from divine ordination, or were it uniquely revealed in the "New Law" of Christ, its justification would be distinctively Christian.

One may, however, distinguish the reasons justifying the moral rule "'S' ought to do 'A'" from the reasons expressed in 'S's intention to do 'A' (and hence explaining or "rationalizing" 'A' when 'S' does 'A' intentionally).[8] In the moral judgment "'S' ought to do 'A'," the *morally relevant description* of 'A' would be distinctively Christian if the description (or intensionally equivalent description) of 'A' that satisfies the judgment, i.e., preserves its validity, implies distinctively Christian reasons for acting, e.g., 'S₁'s promise keeping would be distinctively Christian if the moral description or "content" of 'A' were interpreted as obedience to the divine command.

As we shall see, proponents of both the *Glaubensethik* and the autonomy school err in assuming that the "content" or morally relevant description of 'A' will be distinctively Christian only if the reasons justifying 'A' are logically or epistemically dependent upon Christian belief. The reasons implied in 'A's rationalization or explanation are thus assimilated to the reasons justifying 'A', with the infelicitous consequence of obscuring the *proprium,* or distinctively Christian aspect, of Christian ethics.

The Theological Ethics of Barth and Balthasar

"The foundations of the concept and actuality of obligation," says Barth, are, ab ovo, "christological."[9] In the *pleroma* of Christ's covenant of election, "to 'become obedient,' 'to act rightly,' 'to realize the good,' never means anything other than to become obedient to the revelation of the grace of God; to live as a man to whom grace has come in Jesus Christ." Since there is "no humanity outside the humanity of Jesus Christ," there can be "no realization of the good which is not identical with the grace of Jesus Christ" revealed in the Gospel.[10] Appeals to a natural moral philosophy "originally and ultimately independent of the grace and command of God" must accordingly be renounced as a "perilous distraction."[11] For ethics, as an essentially *theological* inquiry, "is wholly and utterly the knowledge and representation of the Word and work of God."[12]

If "in practice" Christian "insights and deductions may actually exist where their Christian presuppositions are wholly concealed," the *justification* of moral rules can only refer to the ruling and commanding grace of God, which encompasses "all ethical truth": "Correct ethics can only be Christian ethics . . . in a scientific form there is only one ethics, theological ethics." Barth thus denies a "noetic derivation" of moral obligation from Roman Catholic speculation upon nature and the *"anima humana."*[13] For obligation derives from the "sovereign decision of God," the "unconditioned, self-grounded truth which establishes its validity by requiring that we should vindicate ourselves before it."[14] A categorical command, writes Barth, "cannot in the last analysis be merely a command which I have given myself. . . . It must come to me as something alien, as the command of another, demanding as such that I make its content that law of my life." As Anscombe, Barth argues that "[i]f there is an *ought,* it must not be the product of my own will." In establishing "its own validity by asking concerning my own," the divine command, unlike the Kantian imperative, "is a categorical imperative, not merely in name but in fact."[15]

Although commanding grace is "coherent with the one in whom that grace is revealed, and therefore with biblical teaching," Barth contends that the command of God "is given to us at each moment,"

as "not merely a general rule but also a specific prescription and norm
for each individual case."[16] In its historical particularity, the command
of God "does not need any interpretation, for even to the smallest
details it is self-interpreting."[17] The divine command thus assumes
the form of specific, singular imperatives, even as the universal sovereignty of grace offers the promise that all might hear God's gracious
command.

In posing the question "What ought we to do?" Barth asserts
that we are "to do what corresponds to divine grace. We are to respond
to the existence of Jesus Christ and His people." The "ethical problem"
can consist "only in the question whether and to what extent human
action is a glorification of the grace of Jesus Christ."[18] As James Gustafson observes, for Barth ethics "is basically the imitation of God; it is
human action that is in conformity to and bears witness to God's
action" in Christ.[19] "Determined absolutely in the right conduct of
God," morally justifiable action can accordingly be nothing else than
"obedience to God's command." For "the good of human action consists in the fact that it is determined by the divine command."[20] The
morally relevant description of action (implied in the action's justification)
presupposes the "theonomy of human existence," even for those who
fail to perceive it as such.[21] Indeed, "the distinctive essence of all who
live in the world" is "that the decision that has been taken in Jesus
Christ does actually affect them too and their being." Jesus is the
"Lord and Head" of all, "whether they have known him or not," for
they "are only provisionally and subjectively outside Him and without
Him in their ignorance and unbelief."[22] Although morally justifiable
action is implicitly "theonomous," Barth does not presume that the
agent must intend it as such. Yet once the agent seeks to "expose and
expound its presupposition," ethical argument necessarily "becomes
theological ethics." In so affirming the universal sovereignty of God,
Barth denies that the distinctiveness of Christian ethics rests in "special
revelation" or in an "ethics . . . binding only for Church members."[23]

In Barth's dogmatic theology, theonomous *justification* thus generates distinctively Christian *descriptions of moral action* as obedience
to the divine command. One "acts rightly" or "realizes the good" only
if one "becomes obedient to the revelation of the grace of God." For,
avers Barth, "we can never seek the good except in this determination
of human action and therefore in the divine command which creates
this determination in God the commander Himself."[24] Ethics, one
might say, is "Christian" all the way down.

The Glaubensethik *of Hans Urs von Balthasar*

Like Barth, Hans Urs von Balthasar contends that the justification of "Christian ethics . . . comes from and depends on the mystery of Christ."[25] Inspired by Barth's doctrine of a universal predestination, Balthasar depicts Christ as the *universale concretum* of history, the "original model" or "aesthetic" form "of humankind." Everything that, "beside Jesus, still merits a claim on the title 'person' can raise it only on the basis of a relation to him and derivation from him."[26] There is thus no vestibule to moral theology, no purely a priori, transcendental justification of an "anthropological" morality that would reduce revelation to an antecedent rational understanding.[27] For finally it is in the *"Deus absconditus"* of Calvary that the Apollonian charge of *"gnōthi seauton"* is fulfilled; one's freedom comes to term under the banner of a *"theologia crucis."*

As the "form of revelation (*caritas forma revelationis*)," love "(*caritas forma virtutum*) is the fundamental principle of Christian ethics," a love defined supremely in the *kenosis* of Christ.[28] Balthasar tempers Barth's "vivid occasionalism" by recurring to the natural law (as our "natural" ordination to the "transcendental good") but insists, no less than Barth, that Christ is "the concrete categorical imperative," the "plenary norm of all moral action."[29] Embracing "all in their different ethical situations" and uniting "all persons (with their uniqueness and freedom) in his Person," Christ is the "apriori, universal norm" of correct moral conduct.[30]

Balthasar affirms with Barth that "Christian ethics must be elaborated in such a way that its starting point is Jesus Christ." Yet while Barth views "Roman theological ethics" as a Procrustean bed upon which the "primary text" of the Gospel is stretched until it breaks, Balthasar regards the theonomy of human existence as the *telos* of the natural law. Since "the author of grace is also the Creator," writes Balthasar, the "categorical" imperatives of natural law "retain [their] essentially relative character of referring" to "the Absolute Good" without being themselves thereby "divinized."[31] Appeals to natural moral philosophy need not, then, represent an "armistice with the peoples of Canaan," as Barth so feared.[32] For the *logoi* of natural morality "point to the liveliness and self-giving nature of the good," the divine Logos graciously revealed in Christ. The *general* precepts of the natural law, i.e., "first moral principles (*synderesis* or basic conscience)," constitute "the *place* from which the 'positive' revelation of the Old and New Testament has always been addressed to all men."³³ Yet precisely since the divine *telos* of the natural law (the "Absolute Good") is revealed in the divine fidelity of Christ, his "concrete existence"—his "life, suffering, death and bodily resurrection—takes up in itself, supplants and abrogates all other ethical systems." In the "fullness of revelation," the "'Law' and universal 'brotherly love'" appear as but "defective preparatory stages" that "have their 'end' (Rom 10:4) in Christ."³⁴ For Balthasar, the systematic explication of morality bears an ecclesial imprimatur, for "God is disclosed and accessible for us only in Christ; Christ is disclosed and accessible for us only through the Church" (the *"Catholica"*).³⁵

As in Barthian dogmatic theology, the "motive of correct conduct" is finally the "profound revelation of God's holiness" in the covenantal fidelity of Christ. In perfectly fulfilling the divine will, Christ is revealed as the "formal, universal norm of moral life, which can be applied to everyone." The gracious revelation of Christ is "the very condition of [the] possibility" of morally praiseworthy action, so that the *morally relevant description of action* bears implicit reference to the "saving will of God," whether "human beings are explicitly aware of it or not."³⁶ For the Christian, this reference becomes explicit as the "concrete and personal norm" of moral action: just as Barth, Balthasar holds that the reasons *justifying* action recur in the description of the agent's *intentions,* so that "the last end coincides with the first movement of our freedom." Balthasar thus depicts Christ as "the only norm in every situation," for, in "the last analysis, a Christian has to give an account of his moral life only to this norm which proposes the prototype (Jesus) of perfect obedience to God the Father."³⁷

The Autonomy School of Fuchs and Schüller

The rich, almost fugal interweaving of motifs in Balthasar's *Glaubensethik* has seemed "bewildering" to some. "Of course, 'Christ is the categorical imperative in concrete form, in so far as . . . by his suffering . . . he empowers us interiorly to do the Father's will along with him (*cum ipso*),'" concedes Bruno Schüller. Yet such a statement of Christian belief is "completely irrelevant to the question of how, intellectually, we originally know the moral will of God." Indeed, were we to "give this last statement the same logical status that Kant ascribed to the formulations of the categorical imperative, we would be involved in a Christonomous moral positivism."³⁸

Schüller attributes Balthasar's "misunderstanding" to his failure to distinguish scriptural "exhortation" or "paraenesis" from "normative ethics," which is "the object of reason and not of faith." While exhortation retains its "distinct and specific character," the *justification* of moral truth claims is logically independent "of the knowledge which comes through the Judeo-Christian faith."[39] In "the relationship of Gospel to law," there can thus "be no question of normative ethics, that is, of determining and articulating the content of the requirements of morality."[40]

Josef Fuchs argues in a similar vein that "Christian morality in its categorical orientation and materiality is basically and substantially a . . . morality of genuine being-human," which "means that truthfulness, uprightness and faithfulness are not specifically Christian, but generally human values."[41] "The specific and *decisively Christian* aspect of Christian morality is not to be sought" in "categorical values, virtues and norms" as if these descended from the empyrean.[42] Nor is the prescriptive force of moral judgments to be derived from specific divine commands. Finally, Christians and non-Christians alike face "the same epistemological problem, that is to recognize what really is in fact human and what is not, what is or is not a human value. . . . The question is the same for non-Christians and Christians, the criteria for distinguishing between good and bad, honorable and dishonorable, are the same for them as for us."[43]

The *proprium*, or distinctive character, of Christian morality rests not in its material *content*, writes Fuchs, but in its "intentionality" or "motivating power."[44] For "it is . . . also part of the *tradition* of Christian theology that Christ has not added new moral laws to the 'moral codex' of genuine being-human (cf. Thomas Aquinas, Sum. Th. I-II 108, 2)." On the contrary, the "newness that Christ brings is not really a new (material) morality, but the new creature of grace and of the Kingdom of God."[45] Our divine filiation is expressed in the "transcendental" order of intention, which pervades and completes our "particular categorical conduct."[46]

Scripture "speaks unambiguously and frequently about transcendent and Christian attitudes," even as Christian morality remains fundamentally and essentially human in its categorical determination and materiality.[47] What one (morally) ought to do is defined independently of such transcendental attitudes. For distinctive Christian attitudes and beliefs do not contribute to my "categorical" moral obligation to keep my promise to Jones: such *morally relevant descriptions* of actions fall under the banner of the *humanum*.[48] Indeed, even the divine command of *agapē*, fulfilled for Balthasar in "an eschatological, unsurpassable synthesis" in Christ, bears an "autonomous" moral interpretation in the description of moral action. In Schüller's words, "The requirement: 'Do good to others as God has done to you' means, at bottom, 'Act as the golden rule bids you to act,' and this in turn amounts to saying: 'Act in a morally good way.'"[49]

If for Fuchs and Schüller conscience does not make casuists of us all, it is nonetheless divested of distinctive "theonomous" signification. Yet for Barth and Balthasar such "sovereign humanism" represents an attenuation of the moral demands of faith. One wonders, then, if a Christian's faith can be reconciled with the "autonomy" of morality. In the pages that follow, I will seek to show how our hermeneutical analysis of moral action skirts the Scylla of "Christonomous moral positivism" while avoiding the Charybdis of a "fatal assimilation of the Christian to the human."

THE DISTINCTIVENESS OF CHRISTIAN ETHICS

Our conclusions in chapters 5 and 6, Barth or Balthasar might object, betray our allegiance to the autonomy school, for we argued that the ideal of respect for persons admits of a formal, pragmatic justification in which distinctive Christian reasons need not figure. (The very idea of a "theological postscript" would, indeed, be anathema to Barth!) Yet the difficulty, I wish to argue, lies less with the "fatal assimilation of the Christian to the human" than with the semantic confusion of assimilating the varied senses in which an ethics might be "Christian."

Justification

Our reflections upon "intentional" and "moral" actions in chapter 5 permit us to respond to our initial question about the "distinctiveness" of Christian ethics. As we have seen, the *justification* of the moral judgment "'S' ought to do 'A' under the description 'd'" consists in showing that 'A' is fittingly described in terms of a moral maxim and that 'S's intentional performance of 'A' under the (moral) description 'd' satisfies 'S's best reasons, all things considered. The judgment "'S' ought to keep her promise" is justified if her promise keeping falls under a moral maxim specifying her best reasons for acting.

Invocation of the divine command would not, then, define a distinctive set of moral precepts or maxims, as if the sense of the maxim under which 'A' falls were derived theonomously. For were the divine "ought" implied in the description of moral maxims, a logical regression would ensue in which obedience to the divine command is defined in terms of itself. That is, if God commands that 'S' ought to do 'A', and if 'A' is defined *as* "obedience to the divine command," then God commands that 'S' ought to obey that which God commands 'S' ought to obey . . . resulting in the logical indeterminacy of action. No such logical regression is incurred, however, if the divine command ("Thou ought . . . ") is construed as the formal, syntactical requirement of acting in accordance with one's best reason(s), rather than a grammatical remark as to the sense of "ought." God's command might then illumine the morally relevant desirability characteristics of 'A', so that I come to recognize the moral maxim of promise keeping as satisfying my best reasons for acting. Yet if we are to avoid regressive descriptions in which the divine command recurs in the description of what is commanded, the sense of moral maxims must be *logically* independent of the divine command to obey them (i.e., of "theonomy" so construed).

Neither does there seem reason for assuming an *epistemic* (or, in Barth's words, "noetic") dependence of moral maxims upon religious belief. For an agnostic or an atheist incurs moral obligation, e.g., of promise keeping, if she recognizes the pertinent moral maxims in forming her intentions.[50] As we have seen, it suffices for the justification of the moral judgment "'S' ought to do 'A'" that 'A' be fittingly described in terms of 'S's best reasons—even if we offer no further reasons why 'S' should play the practical (moral) language game. The *justification* of moral judgments, we must conclude, is independent, logically and epistemically, of Christian belief. Yet the formal independence or autonomy of moral judgments does not, pace Barth, imply their "original" and "ultimate" independence "of the grace and command of God." Since the justification of a moral judgment (showing *that* it is valid) is logically distinct from a transcendental inquiry into the conditions of the possibility of valid moral judgments (why we play the practical language game), there is no inconsistency in denying the religious dependence of moral justification while affirming the ultimately religious character of our entitlement to moral judgments. One may, that is, offer religious reasons for "being moral" or "playing the moral language game" in affirming the ultimately religious grounds for believing moral reasons are internally predicable of all rational agents, e.g., my belief in promise keeping as a precept enjoined by the respect due persons.

No hubris is implied, then, by the formal requirements of moral justification. For one might assume, in Karl Rahner's words, that the universal "sovereignty of grace" determines the agent's intentional state, as "the objective, ontological modification of man by God's grace" disposing one to adopt a moral point of view, whether explicitly recognized or not.[51] For Rahner and Fuchs, as Gustafson observes, the natural law, which is "knowable and acted upon by all persons," is "Christian and graced because it is created in, by, through, and for Christ, the Incarnate Logos of God."[52] Moral actions attest the "*fides implicita*" of the order of redemption forming "the non-objective and non-specific 'horizon' . . . within which everything of moral and religious . . . significance is contained and ordered to its last end."[53] As our "participation" in the salvific will of God, the natural law, interpreted discursively, might thus be described as the foundation of true theonomous ethics.

The Morally Relevant Description of Action

Our argument thus far supports Fuchs's and Schüller's Rahnerian interpretation, but now we must demur. For Fuchs and Schüller assume that the logical and epistemic independence of moral *justification* from Christian belief implies that the *morally relevant description of action*, in its "categorical orientation and materiality," is basically and substantially a "morality of genuine being-human" (the "Humanum"). The categorically interpreted "content" of moral action is thus distinguished from the "transcendental" order of motive and intention that denominates Christians as such (the "Christianum").

Yet, as we argued in chapter 5, such a simple distinction of motive and content will not suffice. For in accordance with an intensional construal, the "content" or sense of action bears implicit reference to the agent's intention, as did, indeed, "fully human action" for Aristotle and Aquinas: one must do the right deed for the right reason. Lamenting the "great confusion" of the autonomy school's usage of "motive" and "content," Vincent MacNamara observes that "what Fuchs . . . call[s] motives . . . enter into and determine what the agent does—and on any showing should be regarded as the content of the act."[54]

Fuchs might, however, grant the criticism, yet retain the "transcendental" and "categorical" distinction as an internal discrimination of motivation or intention. One may, that is, distinguish "categorical values, virtues and norms," which suffice for the morally relevant description of action, from Christian "transcendental" motivation, which signifies a *further*, paraenetic "motive" or "inspiration" for acting. Reminiscent of Hare, we might thus speak of two orders of interpretation: the "categorical" interpretation of action, referring to general moral norms that explain "what I do" when acting morally, and the "transcendental" interpretation of Christian moral action, supervenient upon the morally relevant description of action. Categorically, Christians and non-Christians appeal, in Fuch's words, to the same "criteria of an ethical epistemology," so that the logical and epistemic independence of the reasons that *justify* moral action pertains, pari passu, to the interpretation of the reasons that *explain* it, i.e., in the morally relevant description of action.

Yet one wonders if this is so. Fuchs himself wavers, arguing that "Christian motivation provides human conduct with a deeper and richer meaning which is subjectively part of the action itself." Indeed, the "'Christianum' . . . not only motivates human conduct more deeply and inspires it, but it will also determine the ways of our conduct *in their content*."[55] The conundrum is resolved, I believe, in our hermeneutical interpretation, for the logical and epistemic independence of moral justification (as detailed in chapters 5 and 6) is entirely consonant with distinctively religious interpretations of moral action: "what *we* do" (as citizens of a kingdom of ends) is abide by the ethical ideal of respect for persons; "what we *do*" in interpreting and applying the ideal of respect in our action will, however, differ across traditions and cultures. Indeed, the abstract generality of moral maxims generates schematic descriptions of action or general action-types that must be further specified by reference to the agent's current attitudes and beliefs, i.e., my belief that performance of 'A' under circumstances 'c' is an instance of the desired action-type, e.g., promise keeping. Since the morally relevant description of 'A' refers to these proximate or "primary reasons" for acting, my intention to do 'A' cannot merely be inferred from my maxim of promise keeping, i.e., that 'A' is fittingly described as fulfilling my promise to Jones.[56]

While numerical distinction of agents $(S_1, S_2, S_3, \ldots S_n)$ does not affect the meaning of moral rules or maxims, e.g., of promise keeping, it is relevant to their application, e.g., whether S_1 ought to keep her promise to S_2 here and now. The universality proper to moral *maxims*, as we saw in our criticism of Kant in chapter 2, must thus be distinguished from the morally relevant description of *actions* in which indexical terms occur, i.e., reference to specific persons, time, place, etc.[57] For although we may recognize the universal maxim of promise keeping, we must still ask if the maxim applies on the occasion of acting: that "I ought to keep my promise to Jones" depends not only upon my recognizing the maxim of promise keeping but upon my belief that I made a promise to Jones, that performing the action 'A' would satisfy my promise, and that no extenuating circumstances obtain.

We must, then, distinguish the moral rules or maxims that may suffice to *justify* an action from the full set of reasons (conative attitudes and beliefs) that *rationalize* it. For, as we argued in chapter 1, the morally relevant description of action is specified by what Aristotle termed the "perception" (*aisthēsis*) of action as an "ultimate *particular*": the agent's "situational appreciation" of the pertinent circumstances of action.[58] Such situational appreciation, as we have seen, reflects distinctive interpretative traditions that illumine the context of acting as, through education and training in virtue (*paideia*), one comes to "see" or, in religious terms, "discern" the morally relevant features of action as "courageous," "just," or "temperate."[59] Instances of justice are thus not merely subsumed as a *casus* of the universal but, rather, exhibit, in Wittgenstein's terms, a "family resemblance" of "overlapping and criss-crossing similarities."[60] Tithing, for instance, represents a distinctive form of promise keeping in certain ecclesial traditions, which *as* promise keeping bears a family resemblance to promise keeping in other cultural, historical, or religious settings.

"Highly specific" scriptural symbols invoked in the application of moral maxims, e.g., the covenant fidelity of Christ, are thus constitutive of morally relevant descriptions of action. Gustafson observes that "religious symbols and theological concepts are used to interpret the moral and religious significance of events and circumstances . . . forming a descriptive evaluation, or evaluative description, of the occasions for action."[61] Although nonreligious or other religious, interpretative settings may contribute to the schematization or "filling in" of moral maxims, one cannot assume that moral actions may be picked out in abstraction from reference to *any* context, as if morality comprised a language of ideal forms. For there is no family resemblance save that exhibited in the varied practices, forms, and traditions of our acting.

Character, virtues, affections thus display their *moral* salience, for they are not to be consigned to the category of motivation, as if they were incidental to the cognitive interpretation of moral content. Our affective dispositions contribute to both the *aisthēsis* or situational appreciation of the occasion of acting and the rationalization of action under the appropriate description. The morphology of Christian morality is accordingly expressed in the interpretation of action, even as the *ultimate* religious grounds for attributing moral reasons to agents may recur in intentional action descriptions.[62] The rationalization or explanation of 'A' may reflect my belief (a) that tithing is a promise that (b) *as* an instance of promise keeping, satisfies my best reasons (c) in accordance with the natural law of divine creation. These beliefs, while logically distinct, generate the morally relevant description of 'A'; for, as Gustafson observes, in "Christian experience of God and its persisting consequences for persons, it is not possible to *separate* the 'religious' characteristics from the 'moral' characteristics of persons."[63]

Neither a simple distinction of moral "intention" or "motive" from "content," as in the autonomy school, nor their uncritical assimilation, as in Balthasar's *Glaubensethik*, will thus finally suffice. For "Christian intentionality" is not supervenient upon the moral action of Christians, as if it were a further motivation—a "transcendental" reason in addition to my categorical reasons for acting. My self-knowledge is, rather, expressed in my having *just* these reasons: in the practical realm, my self-knowledge as a Christian is shown forth in my intention to do 'A', in the explication of which distinctive Christian beliefs may figure. The differing interpretative valences of "Christian" and "moral" in intentional action descriptions permit us to recognize the autonomous role of moral justification while affirming, with Balthasar, the inseparability of the "form" and "content" of Christian *action*, e.g., my tithing in covenantal fidelity as an instance of promise keeping.

The Ontological Difference

Our hermeneutical reflections have the further virtue of clarifying a regrettable obscurity in the writings of Fuchs and Schüller. For although, epistemologically, moral reasons, in Schüller's words, are "inherently accessible to natural reason," a salvific import is imputed to moral action per se, so that the "Humanum" acquires a distinctively religious, indeed Christian significance. Neither Fuchs nor Schüller thus succumbs to Habermas's "rational sublation of theology."[64] For the *epistemological* distinction of transcendental motivation and categorical content is qualified by the *ontological* interpretation of the latter as "implicitly" Christian. Even non-Christians unwittingly exhibit a "transcendent intentionality" in their response to "the gift of grace and to the salvific call"—a response that "animates and permeates [their] categorical moral conduct."[65]

In elaborating his moral theology, Fuchs invokes Rahner's doctrine of the "supernatural existential," i.e., the "objective, ontological modification" of human nature by God's gratuitous self-communication.[66] Nature, one might say, is "charged with the grandeur of God"[67] for, in Rahner's words,

> this absolute eminence is not an optional adjunct to [one's] reality
> . . . it is not given to him as the juridical and external demand
> of God's will for him, but . . . this self-communication by God
> offered to all and fulfilled in the highest way in Christ rather
> constitutes the goal of all creation and—since God's word and
> will *effect* what they say— . . . even before he freely takes up an
> attitude to it, it stamps and determine's man's nature and lends
> it a character which we may call a "supernatural existential."[68]

Even "natural," categorical moral conduct may thus be regarded as implicitly "a response to [God's] call." As John Mahoney remarks apropos of Rahner that,

> just as all . . . who try to live an upright moral life can be re-
> garded, in responding to God's saving grace however implicitly
> or unknowingly, as anonymous Christians, or as saved by "the
> blood of Christ, who through the eternal Spirit offered himself
> without blemish to God (to) purify your conscience from dead
> works to serve the living God" (Heb. 9:14); in like manner all
> true human ethical insights are likewise anonymous Christian
> ethics, or to be considered as exemplifying the theological rich-
> ness of the observation of Ambrosiaster, that "every truth, no
> matter who utters it, has its origin in the Holy Spirit."[69]

Moral and salvific actions are thus coextensive, even if only Christians perceive the distinctively religious ground and goal of creation in the "Humanum." Indeed, for Rahner,

> the categorized explicit love of neighbour is the primary act of the love of God. The love of God unreflectedly but really and always intends God in supernatural transcendentality in the love of neighbour as such, and even the explicit love of God is still borne by that opening in trusting love to the whole of reality which takes place in the love of neighbour.[70]

One's "transcendental" intention reflects the *fides implicita* of moral action "as such," even when the divine horizon within which moral action unfolds remains "unreflected."

Rahner does not thereby deny the significance of religious conversion, for one's "fundamental actuation," in and through love, "like all actuations, cannot and does not want to stop in its anonymous state but strives towards an explicit expression, towards its full name." Neither must we regard the effect of grace:

> as being supernatural in a merely ontic, pre-conscious sense, such as would be required for the positing of any moral act which, as far as consciousness was concerned, was purely natural. Rather must we conceive this grace . . . as also entering consciousness and therefore as engendering true faith in the theological sense, even though this is not yet reflective.[71]

Yet, admirable as the progressively religious (Christian) redescription of action might be, it seems of little *moral* relevance. The thematization of moral action that strives "towards an explicit expression" does not affect our moral epistemology, which, "as far as consciousness was concerned," remains "purely natural." Since the morality of the "Humanum" is defined independently of explicitly religious faith, increments of (Christian) self-knowledge fail to alter the morally relevant description of action. The "categorical" content of moral action is merely subsumed in the generation of Christian redescriptions of moral action. So Fuchs concludes that finally it "does not matter whether or not we call the transcendent intentionality of moral conduct 'Christian' or not." For even the agnostic's moral behavior "signifies true acceptance" of God's "salvific call," whether and to what degree it is expressly thematized.[72]

Yet here, with Stein, we might ask, "What is the question?" For, as Balthasar objects, if "there is ultimately no difference between Christians who are such by name and Christians who are not . . . it cannot matter whether one professes the name or not." Indeed, writes Balthasar, "a person who proclaims the identity of the love of God and one's neighbor and presents the love of one's neighbor as the primary meaning of the love of God must not be surprised (and doubtless is not) if it becomes a matter of indifference whether he professes to believe in God or not."[73] And yet it was precisely the import of this difference—"a deeper and richer *meaning*"—that the "Christianum" sought to illumine.

CONCLUDING REFLECTIONS

Our arguments, I believe, resolve the quandary for, as we have seen, the "deeper and richer" sense of moral action (its ontotheological import for Rahner) is not *epistemologically* nugatory. Inasmuch, indeed, as Christian narrative contributes to the rationalization of moral action (and is not merely supervenient upon it), it is far from a "matter of indifference" whether one professes belief in God in the name of Jesus. For if, as Rahner argues, the effect of grace is not "supernatural in a merely ontic, pre-conscious sense"—if, that is, our moral epistemology is determined *de re* by the "supernatural existential," rather than by the speculative posit of "pure nature"—the denial of the moral relevance of explicitly religious (Christian) consciousness seems "curiouser and curiouser."[74]

Yet the fear that such morally relevant descriptions would imperil the universality and objective validity of moral rules or norms is, we have argued, misplaced: the promise keeping of Christians may be distinctively Christian (i.e., in the generation of appropriate action-descriptions) without thereby ceasing to exemplify the institution of promise keeping. For, as we argued in chapter 1, the "ultimate particularity" of moral action cannot be abstracted from our ethical (*sittlich*) traditions—the "stream of life and thought" in which "what I do" has meaning.[75]

One need not assume, then, that the "majesty of duty" must be vindicated "independently of all experience" (and, a fortiori, of all religious experience). For, as we saw in chapter 2, such a transcendental justification of *Moralität* proved evanescent, leaving Kant's heirs to found morality upon the very hypothetical imperatives he decried as "vain illusion and splendid misery." Yet, as we argued in chapters 3 and 4, neither Hare's "Kantian utilitarianism" nor Rawls's "Kantian contractualism" succeeded in redeeming the "abstract formalism" of Kantian *Moralität*. Indeed, their formal, procedural renderings of justice finally depended upon their differing interpretations of the material criterion of "respect for persons."

Our critical reconstruction of *phronēsis* in chapter 5 set the stage for a retrieval of religious morality as we questioned whether "a moral interpretation of the world" must "escape into some beyond" (the Kantian noumenal realm) for its justification. For if our phronetic "self-knowledge" (as citizens of a possible kingdom of ends) governs the formation of our rationally coherent intentions, Nietzsche's "skepticism regarding morality" need no longer be "decisive." Indeed, as we argued in chapter 6, the "affinity" of our moral self-knowledge and our knowledge of the (common) good, disclosed in "effective reflection," justified our entitlement to objective moral judgment: our common "seeking what is right" (*sunesis*).[76]

Our "Concluding Theological Postscript" thus recalls Sophocles's question at the beginning of our inquiry, "Ah, is there any wisdom in the world?" For our wisdom is "in the world"—not in Habermas's "secular sublation (*Aufhebung*) of ontotheology" but in the "imperfect paradise" of our phronetic judgments (our mundane kingdom of ends).[77] And if here our "explanations run out," in Wittgenstein's words, they do so in a "wise ignorance which knows itself."[78] For in our "flawed words and stubborn sounds" is such grandeur as we know, such solace as we might dream of.

NOTES TO CHAPTER 7

1. Gerard Manley Hopkins, "That Nature Is a Heraclitean Fire and of the Comfort of the Resurrection," in *A Hopkins Reader*, ed. John Pick (Garden City, N.Y.: Image Books, 1966) 80–81.

2. Stanley Hauerwas, *The Peaceable Kingdom: A Primer in Christian Ethics* (Notre Dame: University of Notre Dame Press, 1983), 63.

3. Barth, *Church Dogmatics* II/2, 527.

4. Josef Fuchs, "Is There a Specifically Christian Morality?" in *Readings in Moral Theology*, vol. 2, *The Distinctiveness of Christian Ethics*, ed. Charles Curran and Richard McCormick (New York: Paulist Press, 1980), 4.

5. Bruno Schüller, "The Debate on the Specific Character of Christian Ethics: Some Remarks," in *Readings in Moral Theology*, 2:230. Cf. John Langan,

"Catholic Moral Rationalism and the Philosophical Bases of Moral Theology," *Theological Studies* 50 (1989): 25–43.

6. Aspects of my argument were developed in an earlier essay, "The Distinctiveness of Christian Morality: A Disputed Revisited," *Philosophy & Theology* (forthcoming). I am grateful to the journal for permission to refer to it here.

7. Barth, *Church Dogmatics* II/2, 541; Josef Fuchs, *Natural Law: A Theological Investigation*, trans. by Helmut Reckter and John A. Dowling (New York: Sheed and Ward, 1965), 67.

8. Davidson, *Essays on Actions and Events*, 3–19.

9. Barth, *Church Dogmatics* II/2, 651.

10. Ibid., 539, 541.

11. Ibid., 522, 531.

12. Ibid., 527, 537–38.

13. Ibid., 542, 527, 530–32.

14. Ibid., 652.

15. Ibid., 651–52; cf. G. E. M. Anscombe, "Modern Moral Philosophy," *Philosophy* 33 (1958): 1–19.

16. James Gustafson, *Protestant and Roman Catholic Ethics: Prospects for Rapprochement* (Chicago: University of Chicago Press, 1978), 122; Barth, *Church Dogmatics* II/2, 663.

17. Barth, *Church Dogmatics* II/2, 665.

18. Ibid., 576, 540.

19. Gustafson, *Protestant and Roman Catholic Ethics*, 122.

20. Barth, *Church Dogmatics* II/2, 538, 547. Barth asserts that "we can never seek the good except in this determination of human action and therefore in the divine command which creates this determination in God the commander Himself."

21. Ibid., 526, 542.

22. Barth, *Church Dogmatics* IV/2, trans. G. W. Bromiley (Edinburgh: T. and T. Clark, 1958), 275. For Barth, the domain of moral agents (the *"we* of the ethical question"), while coextensive with "the *we* of the human race," comprises the "highly qualified we of those who—whether they know and believe it or not, whether we can appeal to them on this ground . . . are elected in Jesus Christ to be covenant partners with God." *Church Dogmatics* II/2, 656.

23. Barth, *Church Dogmatics* II/2, 526, 542. In this respect, Barth differs from Hauerwas's narrative ethics.

24. Ibid., 538, 547.

25. Hans Urs von Balthasar, "Nine Theses in Christian Ethics," in *Readings in Moral Theology*, 2:191.

26. Hans Urs von Balthasar, *The Von Balthasar Reader*, ed. Medard Kehland and Werner Löser (New York: Crossroad Publishing Company, 1982), 132.

27. Cf. Hans Urs von Balthasar, *Love Alone*, trans. Alexander Dru (New York: Herder and Herder, 1969), 39, 58.

28. Ibid., 49, 90.

29. Cf. Gustafson's depiction of Barthian epistemology in *Protestant and Roman Catholic Ethics*, 73, 141; Balthasar, "Nine Theses in Christian Ethics," 201, 191.

30. Balthasar, "Nine Theses in Christian Ethics," 193–94.

31. Ibid., 191, 199, 203.

32. Barth, *Church Dogmatics* II/2, 524.

33. Balthasar, "Nine Theses in Christian Ethics," 203.

34. Ibid., 193, 195, 202–203.

35. Balthasar, *The Von Balthasar Reader*, 388. Cf. Barth, *Church Dogmatics* II/2, 527, 541–42.

36. Balthasar, "Nine Theses in Christian Ethics," 199, 191, 195.

37. Ibid., 192–93, 195.

38. Schüller, "The Debate on the Specific Character of a Christian Ethics," 228, 218–19.

39. Ibid., 218, 228, 220, 229–30. Cf. Bruno Schüller, "Zur theologischen Diskussion über die lex naturalis," *Theologie und Philosophie* 41 (1966): 500; and "Die Bedeutung des natürlichen Sittengesetzes für den Christen" in G. Teichtweier, W. Dreier eds., *Herausforderung und Kritik der Moraltheologie* (Würzburg: Echter, 1971), 105.

40. Schüller, "The Debate on the Specific Character of a Christian Ethics," 212.

41. Fuchs, "Is There a Specifically Christian Morality?" 9.

42. Ibid., 5–6.

43. Josef Fuchs, *Human Values and Christian Morality*, trans. M. H. Heelan, Maeve McRedmond, Erika Young, and Gerard Watson (Dublin: Gill and Macmillan, 1970), 121.

44. Ibid., 123–24; "Is There a Specifically Christian Morality?" 14–15.

45. Fuchs, "Is There a Specifically Christian Morality?" 11–12.

46. Ibid., 8.

47. Ibid., 5.

48. Fuchs acknowledges that reason's judgment regarding "historical concrete action is . . . not a pure application of an abstract norm but rather its extensive interpretation." Yet the precise relation of such "extensive interpretation" and the "material content" of the action remains obscure. See Josef Fuchs, "Christliche Moral: Biblische Orientierung und menschliche Wertung," *Stimmen der Zeit* 205 (1987): 682.

49. Schüller, "The Debate on the Specific Character of a Christian Ethics," 210; cf. Fuchs, "Is There a Specifically Christian Morality?" 11–13.

50. Cf. Williams, "Ought and Moral Obligation," 120–21.

51. Karl Rahner and Herbert Vorgrimler, *The Concise Theological Dictionary*, trans. Richard Strachan (Freiburg: Herder, 1965), 178. Cf. Karl Rahner, "Theology and Anthropology," in *Theological Investigations*, vol. 9, trans. Graham Harrison (London: Darton, Longman and Todd, 1973), 28–45.

52. Gustafson, *Protestant and Roman Catholic Ethics*, 118.

53. Rahner and Vorgrimler, *The Concise Theological Dictionary*, 178; cf. Rahner, "Concerning the Relationship Between Nature and Grace," *Theological Investigations*, vol. 1, trans. Cornelius Ernst (London, Darton, Longman and Todd, 1961), 297–317.

54. Vincent MacNamara, *Faith and Ethics: Recent Roman Catholicism* (Washington, D.C.: Georgetown University Press, 1985), 106–107.

55. Fuchs, "Is There a Specifically Christian Morality?" 15.

56. Cf. Davidson, *Essays on Actions and Events*, 5.

57. As Hegel recognized, since the "imperfect duty" of benevolence presupposes a difference of agents' means, benevolent *action* could not be universalized. See G. W. F. Hegel, *Lectures on the History of Philosophy*, trans. Elizabeth S. Haldane and Frances H. Simson (London: Kegan Paul, Trench, Trübner, 1895), 3:460.

58. Aristotle *Nicomachean Ethics* 1143a25–1143b17; David Wiggins, "Deliberation and Practical Reason," 236 (emphasis added).

59. As Stuart Hampshire observes, "The reasons for my actions and conduct, when the actions are voluntary and intended, are to be found in my contemporary desires, current or standing, in my beliefs and knowledge, taken together." My desires "form a vast system" only partially explicated in deliberation, even as my beliefs comprise "a vast store of unsurveyable background knowledge" against which "my specific beliefs about the present situation form themselves." "Public and Private Morality," 30–31.

60. Wittgenstein, *Philosophical Investigations*, pt. 1, par. 66.

61. James Gustafson, *Can Ethics Be Christian?* (Chicago: University of Chicago Press, 1975), 176–77.

62. Ibid.

63. Ibid., 175 (emphasis added).

64. Habermas, *Justification and Application*, 137.

65. Fuchs, "Is There a Specifically Christian Morality?" 18.

66. Rahner and Vorgrimler, *The Concise Theological Dictionary*, 161.

67. Gerard Manley Hopkins, "God's Grandeur," in *A Hopkins Reader*, 47.

68. Rahner, "Anonymous Christians," in *Theological Investigations*, vol. 6, trans. Karl H. and Boniface Kruger (Baltimore: Helicon Press, 1969), 393.

69. John Mahoney, *The Making of Moral Theology: A Study of the Roman Catholic Tradition* (Oxford: Clarendon Press, 1987), 338.

70. Rahner, "Reflections on the Unity of the Love of Neighbour and the Love of God," in *Theological Investigations*, 6:247.

71. Rahner, "Anonymous Christians," 395, 398.

72. Fuchs, "Is There a Specifically Christian Morality?" 18.

73. Hans Urs von Balthasar, *The Moment of Christian Witness*, trans. Richard Beckley (Glen Rock, N.J.: Newman Press, 1969), 71–72.

74. Rahner, "Anonymous Christians," 395, 398. For the *de re* use of definite descriptions, see Saul Kripke, "Naming and Necessity," in *Semantics of Natural Language*, ed. Donald Davidson and Gilbert Harman (Boston: Reidel, 1972), 253–355.

75. Wittgenstein, *Zettel*, par. 173.

76. Gadamer, *Truth and Method*, 323.

77. Habermas, *Justification and Application*, 136; Sophocles *Antigone*, line 1049, p. 154.

78. Wittgenstein, *Philosophical Investigations*, pt. 1, par. 217; Pascal, *Pensées*, (83), 51.

Bibliography

Ackrill, J. L. "Aristotle on Action." In *Essays on Aristotle's Ethics*, ed. Amélie Oksenberg Rorty, 93–101.

———. "Aristotle on *Eudaimonia*." In *Essays on Aristotle's Ethics*, ed. Amélie Oksenberg Rorty, 15–33.

Allan, D. J. "Aristotle's Account of the Origin of Moral Principles." In *Articles on Aristotle: Ethics and Politics*, eds. Jonathan Barnes, Malcolm Schofield, and Richard Sorabji, 72–78.

Ambrosio, Francis J. "Gadamer: On Making Oneself at Home with Hegel." *The Owl of Minerva* 19, no. 1 (1987): 23–40.

Anscombe, G. E. M. "Modern Moral Philosophy." *Philosophy* 33 (1958): 1–19.

———. "Thought and Action in Aristotle." In *Articles on Aristotle: Ethics and Politics*, eds. Jonathan Barnes, Malcolm Schofield, and Richard Sorabji, 61–71.

Aquinas, Thomas. *Summa Theologiae*. Translated by Thomas Gilby. New York: McGraw-Hill, 1964–81.

Aristotle. *Aristotle's Eudemian Ethics*. Translated by Michael Woods. Oxford: Clarendon Press, 1982.

———. *De Amina*. Translated by J. A. Smith. In *The Basic Works of Aristotle*, ed., Richard McKeon.

———. *De Memoria et Reminiscentia*. Translated by J. I. Beare. In *The Basic Works of Aristotle*, ed. Richard McKeon.

———. *Metaphysics*. Translated by W. D. Ross. In *The Basic Works of Aristotle*, ed. Richard McKeon.

———. *Nicomachean Ethics*. Translated by J. A. K. Thomson. Revised by Hugh Tredennick. Harmondsworth, England: Penguin Books, 1976.

———. *Politics*. Translated by T. A. Sinclair. Harmondsworth, England: Penguin Books, 1962.

———. *Rhetoric*. Translated by W. Rhys Roberts. In *The Basic Works of Aristotle*, ed. Richard McKeon.

Balthasar, Hans Urs von. *Love Alone*. Translated by Alexander Dru. New York: Herder and Herder, 1969.

———. *The Moment of Christian Witness*. Translated by Richard Beckley. Glen Rock, N.J.: Newman Press, 1969.

———. "Nine Theses in Christian Ethics." In *Readings in Moral Theology*, vol. 2, eds. Charles Curran and Richard McCormick, 190–206.

————. *The Von Balthasar Reader*. Ed. Medard Kehland and Werner Löser. New York: Crossroad, 1982.

Barker, Ernest. Translator's introduction to *Natural Law and the Theory of Society*, by Otto Gierke. Cambridge: Cambridge University Press, 1958.

Barnes, Jonathan, Malcolm Schofield, and Richard Sorabji, eds. *Articles on Aristotle: Ethics and Politics*. New York: St. Martin's Press, 1978.

Barth, Karl. *Church Dogmatics* II/2. Trans. G. W. Bromiley, J. C. Campbell, Iain Wilson, J. Strathearn McNab, Harold Knight, and R. A. Stewart. Edinburgh: T. and T. Clark, 1957.

————. *Church Dogmatics* IV/2. Translated by G. W. Bromiley. Edinburgh: T and T. Clark, 1958.

Beck, Lewis White. *A Commentary on Kant's Critique of Practical Reason*. Chicago: University of Chicago Press, 1960.

Beckett, Samuel. *Waiting for Godot*. New York: Grove Press, 1954.

Benhabib, Seyla. "The Generalized and the Concrete Other." In *Situating the Self: Gender, Community, and Postmodernism in Contemporary Ethics*, 148–77. New York: Routledge, 1992.

Bentham, Jeremy. *Jeremy Bentham's Economic Writings*. Ed. W. Stark. 3 vols. London: George Allen and Unwin, 1952–54.

Bernstein, Richard. *Beyond Objectivism and Relativism: Science,Hermeneutics, and Praxis*. Philadelphia: University of Pennsylvania Press, 1983.

————. *The New Constellation: The Ethical-Political Horizons of Modernity/Postmodernity*. Cambridge: MIT Press, 1992.

Bernstein, Richard, ed. *Habermas and Modernity*. Cambridge: MIT Press, 1985.

Bleicher, Josef. *Contemporary Hermeneutics: Hermeneutics As Method, Philosophy and Critique*. Boston: Routledge and Kegan Paul, 1980.

Boeckh, August. *Encyklopädie und Methodologie der philologische Wissenschaften*. Ed. Ernst Bratuscheck. Leipzig: Teubner, 1877.

Burke, Edmund. *Reflections on the Revolution in France and on the Proceedings in Certain Societies in London Relative to That Event*. In *Nonsense upon Stilts: Bentham, Burke and Marx on the Rights of Man*, ed. Jeremy Waldron, 96–118. London: Methuen, 1987.

Carroll, Lewis. *The Complete Works of Lewis Carroll*. London: Nonesuch Press, 1939.

Cassirer, Ernst. *Rousseau, Kant, Goethe: Two Essays*. Trans. James Gutman, Paul Oskar Kristeller, and John Herman Randall, Jr. Princeton: Princeton University Press, 1945.

Catullus. *The Poems of Catullus*. Trans. Peter Whigham. Baltimore: Penguin Books, 1966.

Coleman, John. "Catholic Human Rights Theory: Four Challenges to an Intellectual Tradition." *Journal of Law and Religion* 2 (1984): 343–66.

Curran, Charles, and Richard McCormick eds. *Readings in Moral Theology: The Distinctiveness of Christian Ethics*. Vol. 2. New York: Paulist Press, 1980.

Dallmayr, Fred, and Thomas A. McCarthy, eds. *Understanding and Social Inquiry*. Notre Dame: University of Notre Dame Press, 1977.

Daniels, Norman, ed. *Reading Rawls*. New York: Basic Books, 1975.

Davidson, Donald. *Essays on Actions and Events*. Oxford: Clarendon Press, 1980.

———. *Inquiries into Truth and Interpretation*. Oxford: Clarendon Press, 1984.

———. "Replies to Essays I-X." In *Essays on Davidson: Actions and Events*, ed. Bruce Vermazen and Merrill B. Hintikka. Oxford, Clarendon Press, 1985.

d'Entrèves, A. P. *Natural Law*. 2d ed. London: Huchinson and Company, 1970.

Donagan, Alan. *The Theory of Morality*. Chicago: University of Chicago Press, 1977.

Donne, John. "An Anatomy of the World." In *The Complete English Poems*, ed. A. J. Smith. New York: Penguin Books, 1971.

Dumont, Louis. "The Modern Conception of the Individual: Notes on Its Genesis and That of Concomitant Institutions." *Contributions to Indian Sociology*, 8 (October 1965), 13–61.

Dupré, Louis. *A Dubious Heritage: Studies in the Philosophy of Religion After Kant*. New York: Paulist Press, 1977.

Dworkin, Ronald. *Taking Rights Seriously*. Cambridge: Harvard University Press, 1978.

Eliot, T. S. "Gerontion." In *The Complete Poems and Plays*. New York: Harcourt, Brace and World, 1958.

———. "The Hollow Men." In *The Complete Poems and Plays*.

———. "Journey of the Magi." In *The Complete Poems and Plays*.

———. "The Love Song of J. Alfred Prufrock." In *The Complete Poems and Plays*.

———. *Murder in the Cathedral*. In *The Complete Poems and Plays*.

———. "Tradition and the Individual Talent." In *Criticism: The Major Texts*, ed. Walter Jackson Bate. New York: Harcourt, Brace and World, 1952.

———. "The Waste Land." In *The Complete Poems and Plays*.

Ellacuría, Ignacio. "Human Rights in a Divided Society." In *Human Rights in the Americas: The Struggle for Consensus*, ed. Alfred Hennelly and John Langan, 52–65. Washington, D.C.: Georgetown University Press, 1982.

Foot, Philippa. "Morality as a System of Hypothetical Imperatives. In *Virtues and Vices*. Oxford: Basil Blackwell, 1978.

———. "A Reply to Professor Frankena." In *Virtues and Vices*.

Foster, Matthew. *Gadamer and Practical Philosophy: The Hermeneutics of Moral Confidence*. Atlanta: Scholars Press, 1991.

Frankfurt, Harry. "Freedom of the Will and the Concept of a Person." *Journal of Philosophy* 68, no. 1 (1971): 5–20.

Frege, Gottlob. "On Sense and Meaning." In *Translations from the Philosophical Writings of Gottlob Frege*, ed. Peter Geach and Max Black, 56–78. 3d ed. Oxford: Basil Blackwell, 1980.

Fuchs, Josef. *Christian Ethics in a Secular Arena*. Washington, D.C.: Georgetown University Press, 1984.

———. "Christliche Moral: Biblische Orientierung und menschliche Wertung" *Stimmen der Zeit* 205 (1987): 671–84.

———. *Human Values and Christian Morality*. Trans. M. H. Heelan, Maeve McRedmond, Erika Young, and Gerard Watson. Dublin: Gill and Macmillan, 1970.

———. "Is There A Specifically Christian Morality?" In *Readings in Moral Theology: The Distinctiveness of Christian Ethics*, eds. Charles Curran and Richard McCormick, vol. 2, 3–19.

———. *Natural Law: A Theological Investigation*. Trans. Helmut Reckter and John A. Dowling. New York: Sheed and Ward, 1965

Gadamer, Hans-Georg. *Dialogue and Dialectic: Eight Hermeneutical Studies on Plato*. Trans. by P. Christopher Smith. New Haven: Yale University Press, 1980.

———. *Hegel's Dialectic: Five Hermeneutical Studies*. Trans. P. Christopher Smith. New Haven: Yale University Press, 1976.

———. *The Idea of the Good in Platonic-Aristotelian Philosophy*. Trans. P. Christopher Smith. New Haven: Yale University Press, 1986.

———. *Philosophical Hermeneutics*. Trans. and ed. David E. Linge. Berkeley: University of California Press, 1976.

———. "The Problem of Historical Consciousness." Trans. Jeff. L. Close. In *Interpretative Social Science: A Reader*, ed. Paul Rabinow and William M. Sullivan, 103–60. Berkeley: University of California Press, 1979.

———. *Reason in the Age of Science*. Trans. Frederick G. Lawrence. Cambridge: MIT Press, 1981.

———. *The Relevance of the Beautiful and Other Essays*. Trans. Nicholas Walker. Cambridge: Cambridge University Press, 1986.

———. *Truth and Method*. Trans. Joel Weinsheimer and Donald G. Marshall. 2d ed. New York: Crossroad 1991.

Gay, Peter, ed. *The Enlightenment: A Comprehensive Anthology*. New York: Simon and Schuster, 1973.

Gewirth, Alan. *Reason and Morality*. Chicago: University of Chicago Press, 1978.

Gierke, Otto. *Natural Law and the Theory of Society, 1500–1800*. Trans. E. Barker. Cambridge: Cambridge University Press, 1958.

Gustafson, James. *Can Ethics Be Christian?* Chicago: University of Chicago Press, 1975.

———. *Protestant and Roman Catholic Ethics: Prospects for Rapprochement*. Chicago: University of Chicago Press, 1978.

Habermas, Jürgen. "The Hermeneutic Claim to Universality." Trans. Josef Bleicher. In *Contemporary Hermeneutics: Hermeneutics as Method, Philosophy, and Critique*, by Josef Bleicher, 181–211.

———. *Justification and Application: Remarks on Discourse Ethics*. Trans. Ciaran P. Cronin. Cambridge: MIT Press, 1993.

———. *Knowledge and Human Interests*. Trans. Jeremy J. Shapiro. Boston: Beacon Press, 1971.

———. *Moral Consciousness and Communicative Action*. Trans. Christian Lenhardt and Shierry Weber Nicholsen. Cambridge: MIT Press, 1990.

———. *The Philosophical Discourse of Modernity*. Trans. Frederick Lawrence. Cambridge: MIT Press, 1987.

———. "A Philosophico-Political Profile." In *Habermas: Autonomy and Solidarity*, ed. and trans. Peter Dews. London: New Left Books, 1986.

———. *Postmetaphysical Thinking: Philosophical Essays*. Translated by William Mark Hohengarten. Cambridge: MIT Press, 1992.

———. "A Review of Gadamer's *Truth and Method*." In *Understanding and Social Inquiry*, ed. Fred R. Dallmayr and Thomas A. McCarthy, 335–63. Notre Dame: University of Notre Dame Press, 1977.

———. "On Systematically Distorted Communication." *Inquiry* 13 (1970): 205–18.

———. *The Theory of Communicative Action*. Trans. Thomas McCarthy. 2 vols. Boston: Beacon Press, 1981.

———. "Toward a Theory of Communicative Competence." *Inquiry* 13 (1970): 360–75.

Hampshire, Stuart. "Public and Private Morality." In *Public and Private Morality*, ed. Stuart Hampshire, 23–54. Cambridge: Cambridge University Press, 1978.

Hare, R. M. "Do Agents Have to Be Moralists?" In *Gewirth's Ethical Rationalism: Critical Essays with a Reply by Alan Gewirth*, ed. Edward Regis, Jr., 52–58. Chicago: University of Chicago Press, 1984.

———. "Ethical Theory and Utilitarianism." In *Utilitarianism and Beyond*, ed. Amartya Sen and Bernard Williams, 23–38.

———. *Freedom and Reason*. Oxford: Oxford University Press, 1963.

———. *Moral Thinking*. Oxford: Oxford University Press, 1981.

———. "Rawls' Theory of Justice." In *Reading Rawls*, ed. Norman Daniels, 81–107.

———. "Rights, Utility, and Universalization: Reply to J. L. Mackie." In *Utility and Rights*, ed. R. G. Frey, 106–20. Minneapolis: University of Minnesota Press, 1984.

Hauerwas, Stanley. *The Peaceable Kingdom: A Primer in Christian Ethics*. Notre Dame: University of Notre Dame Press, 1983.

Hegel, G. W. F. *Hegel's Phenomenology of Spirit*. Trans. A. V. Miller. Oxford: Oxford University Press, 1977.

———. *Hegel's Philosophy of Right*. Trans. T. M. Knox. Oxford: Oxford University Press, 1952.

———. *Lectures on the History of Philosophy*. 3 vols. Trans. Elizabeth S. Haldane and Frances H. Simson. London: Kegan Paul, Trench, Trübner, 1892–96.

Heidegger, Martin. *Being and Time*. Trans. John Macquarrie and Edward Robinson. New York: Harper and Row, 1962.

———. "Hölderlin and the Essence of Poetry." Trans. Douglas Scott. In *Existence and Being*, ed. Werner Brock. Chicago: Henry Regnery, 1949, 270–91.

———. "Letter on Humanism." Trans. Frank A. Capuzzi and J. Glenn Gray. In *Martin Heidegger: Basic Writings*, ed. David Farrell Krell. New York: Harper and Row, 1977, 193–242.

Held, David, and John B. Thompson, eds. *Habermas: Critical Debates*. Cambridge: MIT Press, 1982.

Henrich, Dieter. "The Proof-Structure of Kant's Transcendental Deduction." *Review of Metaphysics* 22 (June, 1969): 640–59.

Hobbes, Thomas. *Human Nature: Or the Fundamental Elements of Policy*. In *British Moralists, 1650–1800*, vol. 1, ed. D. D. Raphael, 3–17.

———. *Leviathan*. Ed. C. B. Macpherson. Baltimore: Penguin Books, 1968.

———. *Of Liberty and Necessity*. In *British Moralists, 1650–1800*, vol. 1, ed. D. D. Raphael, 61–70.

Hollenbach, David. "The Common Good Revisited." *Theological Studies* 50 (1989): 70–94.

Hopkins, Gerard Manley. "God's Grandeur." In *A Hopkins Reader*, ed. John Pick. Garden City, N.Y.: Image Books, 1966.

———. "That Nature Is a Heraclitean Fire and of the Comfort of the Resurrection." In *A Hopkins Reader*, 80–81.

Hume, David. *An Inquiry Concerning the Principles of Morals*. Ed. Charles W. Hendel. New York: Macmillan, 1957.

———. *A Treatise of Human Nature*. In *British Moralists, 1650–1800*, vol. 2, ed. D. D. Raphael, 3–58.

Husserl, Edmund. *The Crisis of European Sciences and Transcendental Phenomenology*. Trans. David Carr. Evanston, Ill.: Northwestern University Press, 1970.

Hutcheson, Francis. *An Essay on the Nature and Conduct of the Passions and Affections*. In *British Moralists, 1650–1800*, vol. 1, ed. D. D. Raphael, 300–304.

Kant, Immanuel. *Critique of Judgment*. Trans. J. H. Bernard. New York: Hafner Press, 1951.

———. *Critique of Practical Reason*. Trans. Lewis White Beck. Indianapolis: Bobbs-Merrill, 1956.

———. *Critique of Pure Reason*. Trans. Norman Kemp Smith. New York: St. Martin's Press, 1929.

———. *Groundwork of the Metaphysic of Morals*. Trans. H. J. Paton. New York: Harper and Row, 1964.

———. *Lectures on Ethics*. Trans. Louis Infield. Indianapolis: Hackett Publishing Company, 1963.

———. *The Metaphysical Elements of Justice*, Pt. 1 of the *Metaphysics of Morals*. Trans. John Ladd. Indianapolis: Bobbs-Merrill, 1965.

———. *The Metaphysics of Morals*. Trans. Mary Gregor. Cambridge: Cambridge University Press, 1991.

———. *Religion within the Limits of Reason Alone*. Trans. Theodore M. Greene and Hoyt H. Hudson. New York: Harper and Row, 1960.

Kierkegaard, Søren. *Concluding Unscientific Postscript*. Trans. David F. Swenson and Walter Lowrie. Princeton: Princeton University Press, 1941.

Kneale, Martha and William Kneale. *The Development of Logic*. Oxford: Clarendon Press, 1962.

Körner, Stephan. *Kant*. New Haven: Yale University Press, 1955.

Kripke, Saul. "Naming and Necessity." In *Semantics of Natural Language*, ed. Donald Davidson and Gilbert Harman, 253–355. Boston: Reidel, 1972.

Kuhn, T. S. "Reflections on My Critics." In *Criticism and the Growth of Knowledge*, ed. I. Lakatos and A. Musgrave. Cambridge: Cambridge University Press, 1970.

Langan, John. "Catholic Moral Rationalism and the Philosophical Bases of Moral Theology." *Theological Studies* 50 (1989): 25–43.

Linge, David. Editor's introduction to *Philosophical Hermeneutics*, by Hans-Georg Gadamer. Berkeley: University of California Press, 1976.

Lukes, Steven. *Individualism*. Oxford: Basil Blackwell, 1973.

MacIntyre, Alasdair. *After Virtue*. 2d ed. Notre Dame: University of Notre Dame Press, 1984.

Mackie, John L. *Ethics: Inventing Right and Wrong*. Harmondsworth, England: Penguin, 1978.

MacNamara, Vincent. *Faith and Ethics: Recent Roman Catholicism*. Washington D.C.: Georgetown University Press, 1985.

Mahoney, John. *The Making of Moral Theology: A Study of the Roman Catholic Tradition*. Oxford: Clarendon Press, 1987.

Maritain, Jacques. "The Person and the Common Good." In *The Social and Political Philosophy of Jacques Maritain*, ed. Joseph W. Evans and Leo R. Ward. New York: Charles Scribner's Sons, 1955.

McKeon, Richard, ed. *The Basic Works of Aristotle*. New York: Random House, 1941.

Melden, A.I. *Rights in Moral Lives*. Berkeley: University of California Press, 1988.

Nagel, Thomas. "Rawls on Justice." In *Reading Rawls*, ed. Norman Daniels, 1–17.

Nietzsche, Friedrich. *The Will to Power*. Bk. 1. Translated by W. Kaufmann. In *Existentialism from Dostoevsky to Sartre*, by W. Kaufman, 100–101. New York: Meridian Books, 1956.

Pascal, Blaise. *Pensées*. Translated by A. J. Krailsheimer. Harmondsworth, England: Penguin Books, 1966.

Paton, H. J. *The Categorical Imperative: A Study in Kant's Moral Philosophy*. Philadelphia: University of Pennsylvania Press, 1948.

Pico della Mirandola. *Oration on the Dignity of Man*. In "The Philosophy of Man in the Italian Renaissance," by P. O. Kristeller. *Italica* 24 (1947): 93–112.

Plato. *Theaetetus*. Trans. Francis M. Cornford. New York: The Liberal Arts Press, 1959.

Quine, W. V. "Speaking of Objects." In *Ontological Relativity and Other Essays*. New York: Columbia University Press, 1969.

———. "Two Dogmas of Empiricism." In *From a Logical Point of View*, 2d ed. Cambridge: Harvard University Press, 1961.

Rahner, Karl. "Anonymous Christians." In *Theological Investigations*, vol. 6, Trans. Karl H. and Boniface Kruger. Baltimore: Helicon Press, 1969.

———. "Concerning the Relationship between Nature and Grace." In *Theological Investigations*. vol. 1, Trans. Cornelius Ernst. London, Darton, Longman and Todd, 1961.

————. "Reflections on the Unity of the Love of Neighbour and the Love of God." In *Theological Investigations*, vol. 6.

————. "Theology and Anthropology." In *Theological Investigations*, vol. 9. Trans. Graham Harrison. London: Darton, Longman and Todd, 1973.

Rahner, Karl, and Herbert Vorgrimler. *The Concise Theological Dictionary*. Trans. Richard Strachan. Freiburg: Herder, 1965.

Raphael, D. D. ed. *British Moralists, 1650–1800*. 2 vols. Oxford: Clarendon Press, 1969.

Rawls, John. "The Basic Structure As Subject." *American Philosophical Quarterly* 14 (1977): 159–65.

————. "Fairness to Goodness." *Philosophical Review* 84 (1975): 536–54.

————. "Kantian Constructivism in Moral Theory." *Journal of Philosophy* 77, no. 9 (1980): 515–72.

————. *Political Liberalism*. New York: Columbia University Press, 1993.

————. "Social Unity and Primary Goods." In *Utilitarianism and Beyond*, ed. Amartya Sen and Bernard Williams, 159–85.

————. *A Theory of Justice*. Cambridge: Harvard University Press, Belknap Press, 1971.

————. "A Well-Ordered Society." In *Philosophy, Politics, and Society*, 5th ser., ed. P. Laslett and J. Fishkin, 6–20. New Haven: Yale University Press, 1979.

Ricoeur, Paul. "Hermeneutics and the Critique of Ideology." In *Hermeneutics and the Human Sciences: Essays on Language, Action and Interpretation*, ed. and trans. John B. Thompson. Cambridge: Cambridge University Press, 1981.

Rorty, Amélie Oksenberg, ed. *Essays on Aristotle's Ethics*. Berkeley: University of California Press, 1980.

Rorty, Richard. "The Priority of Democracy to Philosophy." In *Prospects for a Common Morality*, ed. Gene Outka and John Reeder, 254–78. Princeton: Princeton University Press, 1993.

Ross, David. *The Right and the Good*. Oxford: Clarendon Press, 1930.

Rousseau, Jean-Jacques. *The Creed of a Priest of Savoy*. Translated by Arthur H. Beattie. 2d ed. New York: Frederick Ungar, 1957.

————. *The Social Contract*. Translated by Maurice Cranston. Harmondsworth, Middlesex: Penguin Books, 1968.

Sandel, Michael J. *Liberalism and the Limits of Justice*. Cambridge: Cambridge University Press, 1982.

Sartre, Jean-Paul. *Existentialism and Humanism*. Trans. Philip Mairet. London: Methuen, 1948.

Sen, Amartya, and Bernard Williams, eds. *Utilitarianism and Beyond*. Cambridge: Cambridge University Press, 1982.

Schüller, Bruno. "Die Bedeutung des natürlichen Sittengesetzes für den Christen." In *Herausforderung und Kritik der Moraltheologie*, eds. G. Teichtweier and W. Dreier, 481–503. Würzburg: Echter, 1971.

————. "The Debate on the Specific Character of Christian Ethics: Some Remarks." In *Readings in Moral Theology: The Distinctiveness of Christian Ethics*, vol. 2, ed. Charles Curran and Richard McCormick, 207–33.

————. "Zur theologischen Diskussion über die lex naturalis," *Theologie und Philosophie* 41 (1966): 481–503.

Shapiro, Gary, and Alan Sica, eds. *Hermeneutics: Questions and Prospects*. Amherst: University of Massachusetts Press, 1984.

Shue, Henry. *Basic Rights: Subsistence, Affluence, and U.S. Foreign Policy*. Princeton: Princeton University Press, 1980.

Sidgwick, Henry. *The Methods of Ethics*. 7th ed. Indianapolis: Hackett, 1981.

Silverman, Hugh J. ed. *Gadamer and Hermeneutics*. New York: Routledge, 1991.

Sophocles. *The Theban Plays*. Translated by E. F. Watling. Baltimore: Penguin Books, 1947.

Stevens, Wallace. "Adagia." In *Opus Posthumous*, ed. Samuel French Morse. New York: Alfred A. Knopf, 1957.

————. "Asides on the Oboe." In *The Palm at the End of the Mind*, ed. Holly Stevens. New York: Vintage Books, a Division of Random House, 1971.

————. "The Poems of Our Climate." In *The Palm at the End of the Mind*. New York: Random House, 1972.

Strauss, Leo. *Natural Right and History*. Chicago: University of Chicago Press, 1953.

Tarski, A. "The Semantic Conception of Truth." *Philosophical and Phenomenological Research* 4 (1944): 341–75.

Taylor, Charles. "The Concept of a Person." In *Philosophical Papers*, vol. 1, 97–114. Cambridge: Cambridge University Press, 1985.

————. *Sources of the Self: The Making of the Modern Identity*. Cambridge: Harvard University Press, 1989.

Vico, Giambattista. *On the Study of Methods of Our Time*. Trans. Elio Gianturco. Indianapolis: Bobbs-Merrill, 1965.

Warnke, Georgia. *Gadamer: Hermeneutics, Tradition and Reason*. Stanford: Stanford University Press, 1987.

Weber, Max. "Science as a Vocation." In *From Max Weber: Essays in Sociology*, ed. H. H. Gerth and C. W. Mills, 77–128. New York: Oxford University Press, 1946.

Weinsheimer, Joel C. *Gadamer's Hermeneutics: A Reading of Truth and Method*. New Haven: Yale University Press, 1985.

Wiggins, David. "Deliberation and Practical Reason." In *Essays on Aristotle's Ethics*, ed. Amélie Oksenberg Rorty, 221–40.

————. "Weakness of Will, Commensurability, and the Objects of Deliberation and Desire." In *Essays on Aristotle's Ethics*, ed. Amélie Oksenberg Rorty, 241–265.

Williams, Bernard. "A Critique of Utilitarianism." In *Utilitarianism: For and Against*, ed. J. J. C. Smart and Bernard Williams, 75–155. Cambridge: Cambridge University Press, 1973.

————. *Ethics and the Limits of Philosophy*. Cambridge: Harvard University Press, 1985.

————. *Moral Luck: Philosophical Papers, 1973–1980*. Cambridge: Cambridge University Press, 1981.

————. *Problems of the Self: Philosophical Papers, 1956–1972*. Cambridge: Cambridge University Press, 1973.

Wittgenstein, Ludwig. *On Certainty*. Trans. Denis Paul and G. E. M. Anscombe. New York: Harper and Row, 1969.

——. *Philosophical Investigations*. Trans. G. E. M. Anscombe. 3d ed. New York: Macmillan, 1968.

——. *Tractatus Logio-Philosophicus*. Trans. D. F. Pears and B. F. McGuinness. London: Routledge and Kegan Paul, 1922.

——. *Zettel*. Trans. G. E. M. Anscombe. Oxford: Basil Blackwell, 1967.

Yeats, William Butler. "The Second Coming." In *The Collected Poems of W. B. Yeats*. New York: Macmillan, 1956.

Young, Iris Marion. "Impartiality and the Civic Public." In *Feminism as Critique*, ed. Seyla Benhabib and Drucilla Cornell, 57–76. Minneapolis: University of Minnesota Press, 1987.

Zeller, Eduard. *Aristotle and the Earlier Peripatetics*. Trans. B. F. C. Costelloe and J. H. Muirhead. Vol. 2. New York: Russell and Russell, 1962.

Index